DIVORCE

by

JOHN MURRAY

Professor of Systematic Theology
Westminster Theological Seminary
Philadelphia, Pennsylvania

PRESBYTERIAN AND REFORMED PUBLISHING CO.
Phillipsburg, New Jersey

ISBN: 0-87552-344-7

PRINTED IN THE UNITED STATES OF AMERICA

Foreword

I am grateful to the Presbyterian and Reformed Publishing Company for undertaking to publish these studies on the subject of divorce in a new format. With the exception of the indices the edition of 1953 by the Committee on Christian Education of the Orthodox Presbyterian Church is herewith reproduced. It would be desirable to expand these studies. But under present circumstances extensive revision is not feasible. Besides, I do not find it necessary to alter the positions taken in the earlier publications. Subsequent study and the numerous practical cases brought to my attention in the intervening years have tended rather to confirm the conclusions which were first given to the public in six issues of *The Westminister Theological Journal* from 1946 to 1949. Hence revision would have to be in the form of elaboration rather than of substantial modification. Although certain developments of thought and practice call for further treatment, yet the principles in terms of which these are to be evaluated remain the same and it does not appear to me mandatory to incorporate this new material.

The church of Christ is being increasingly perplexed by marital situations which in one way or another are related to divorce. Pastors and those in whom government is vested know only too well how complex many of these cases are and what heart burning they entail for them. Any tendency to allow sociological considerations divorced from biblical teaching to dictate advice or solution is unworthy of the church of Christ. It is necessary to prize ever and anon the infallible rule of faith and practice provided for us in Holy Scripture.

The indices for the current edition (1961) have been prepared by Mr. Duncan Lowe of Long Island, New York.

JOHN MURRAY

Philadelphia
March 11, 1961

Contents

Preface

The question of divorce is one that perennially interests and agitates the church. This is true whether we think of the church in the most restricted sense as the local congregation or whether we think in terms of the church universal. The faithful pastor of the local church may consider himself happy indeed if he does not find himself embroiled in the complications associated with divorce and marital separations. And when we consider the matter more broadly we find deep-seated differences of viewpoint and interpretation within the historic branches of the Christian church.

It would be presumptuous to claim that a study such as is now being undertaken will resolve the many difficult questions involved. Nevertheless a better understanding of the teaching of Scripture may be promoted if the pivotal passages are discussed in correlation with one another and some attempt is made to bring the relevant Biblical data to the forefront for reflection and study.

It is quite apparent that the first biblical passage bearing upon the question is Genesis 2:23, 24. At the very outset this enunciates the nature and basis of marriage and clearly implies that divorce or the dissolution of the marriage bond could not be contemplated otherwise than as a radical breach of the divine institution. It is impossible to envisage any dissolution of the bond as anything other than abnormal and evil. Our Lord's comments with reference to this Scripture and the institution underlying it are to the effect of showing that the marriage bond is originally and ideally indissoluble. The rupture of this divinely instituted human bond is conceivable only if there is first of all the rupture of divine-human relations. The breach of the divinely instituted order of right and troth and love in the human sphere must presuppose the breach of troth with God.

1

This breach of troth with God did, of course, occur in the fall. It was not indeed through the desecration of the marriage bond that sin entered. It was by another avenue. But since sin did enter the question naturally arises: how does the abnormal situation created by sin affect the marital relation? A new complex of conditions and circumstances enters by sin and since sin desecrates all relationships we are bound to face the question of the bearing of sin upon the sanctity of the marriage bond. Granting the basic and original principle of the indissolubility of the marriage bond, yet, by reason of sin, are there any conditions under which the marriage tie may be dissolved with divine sanction and authorisation?

When we ask this question we must never forget that the sinful situation which compels us to raise the question is one that rests under the divine judgment. In like manner the specific conditions which might require or warrant the dissolution of the marriage bond must be regarded as resting under the condemnation of God. Yet, presupposing divine condemnation of the sinful situation in its totality and of the specifically sinful condition that might provide the ground for divorce, it is still possible to envisage a divinely authorised and instituted right of divorce. It is quite conceivable that while the reason for divorce is sinful the right of divorce for that reason may be divine.

The cardinal passages of Scripture upon which any treatment of the Biblical teaching must turn are: Deuteronomy 24:1–4; Matthew 5:31, 32; 19:3–12; Mark 10:2–12; Luke 16:18; I Corinthians 7:15; Romans 7:1–3. Our study will, therefore, be largely occupied with the interpretation of these passages.

I

The Old Testament Provision

This passage occupies a unique place in the Old Testament because it contains, as no other passage in the Old Testament, specific legislation bearing upon the question of divorce. The references to this passage in both Testaments confirm the significance that attaches to it in the Old Testament economy (*cf.* Isa. 50:1; Jer. 3:1; Matt. 5:31; Matt. 19:7, 8; Mark 10:3–5).

The understanding of the import of this passage has been perplexed, if not distorted, by the adoption of a translation which, though possible, is not by any means the most defensible. This translation has been followed by the Authorised, Revised and American Revised Versions in English. The Authorised reads as follows:

> When a man hath taken a wife, and married her, and it come to pass that she find no favour in his eyes, because he hath found some uncleanness in her: then let him write her a bill of divorcement, and give *it* in her hand, and send her out of his house.
>
> 2. And when she is departed out of his house, she may go and be another man's *wife*.
>
> 3. And *if* the latter husband hate her, and write her a bill of divorcement, and giveth *it* in her hand, and sendeth her out of his house; or if the latter husband die, which took her *to be* his wife;
>
> 4. Her former husband, which sent her away, may not take her again to be his wife, after that she is defiled; for that *is* abomination before the Lord: and thou shalt not cause the land to sin, which the Lord thy God giveth thee *for* an inheritance.

The crucial point to be noted in this rendering is that the apodosis to the protasis expressed in the first part of verse 1 begins at the middle of the same verse and reads, "then let him write her a bill of divorcement, and give it in her hand, and send her out of his house". On this rendering the divorce could well be construed as mandatory in the circumstance posited. No doubt many English readers have understood the passage in this way and so have regarded divorce as commanded in the event of the uncleanness mentioned in the protasis of the sentence. The inference would naturally be that not only was divorce permitted in this case but was also prescribed.

The English Revised and American Revised Versions alter the rendering of verse 1 and might possibly be interpreted as toning down the mandatory feature that is prominent in the translation of the Authorised Version. They both translate verse 1 as follows:

> When a man taketh a wife, and marrieth her, then it shall be, if she find no favour in his eyes, because he hath found some unseemly thing in her, that he shall write her a bill of divorcement, and give it in her hand, and send her out of his house.

While the apodosis in this case is introduced earlier than in the case of the Authorised Version and while the English reader might not be so ready to give mandatory force to the rendering, careful examination of the construction would lead the reader to understand that the husband in this case was required to give his wife a bill of divorcement, give it in her hand and send her out of his house. And the English reader would still be justified in regarding this piece of Mosaic legislation as not only permitting divorce, in the case of the uncleanness mentioned, but as also requiring it.[1]

---

[1] It is the presence of the word "shall" in both clauses — "then it shall be ... that he shall write her a bill of divorcement" — that lends to the rendering of both the Revised and the American Revised Versions the jussive force. If a rendering similar to that of Joseph Reider had been adopted the jussive feature would have been eliminated, even though the form of the translation would not have been materially altered — "when a man taketh a wife, and marrieth her, then it cometh to pass, if she find no favor in his eyes, because he hath found some unseemly thing in her, that he writeth her a bill of divorcement, and giveth it in her hand, and sendeth her out of his house" etc. (*Deuteronomy with Commentary*, Philadelphia, 1937, pp. 220 f.).

What should be recognised and appreciated is that this type of rendering and the view regarding the syntax that underlies it are quite unnecessary and are not supported by scholars and commentators whose judgment in this matter is worthy of the greatest deference.

It is significant that Calvin in his comments on the passage in question recognises the precise point which has been raised by the construction of the passage. He says: "Some interpreters do not read these three verses continuously, but suppose the sense to be complete at the end of the first, wherein the husband testifies that he divorces his wife for no offence, but because her beauty does not satisfy his lust. If, however, we give more close attention, we shall see that it is only one provision of the Law, viz., that when a man has divorced his wife, it is not lawful for him to marry her again if she have married another."[2]

More modern scholars, also, of various theological viewpoints are insistent that the protasis in this passage embraces the first three verses and that it is only at the beginning of verse 4 that the apodosis is introduced.

The comment of C. F. Keil and F. Delitzsch brings out this construction very clearly: "In these verses . . . divorce is not established as a right; all that is done is, that in case of a divorce a reunion with the divorced wife is forbidden, if in the meantime she had married another man, even though the second husband had also put her away, or had died. The four verses form a period, in which vers. 1–3 are the clauses of the protasis, which describe the matter treated about; and ver. 4 contains the apodosis, with the law concerning the point in question."[3] S. R. Driver says with reference to this passage: "The rend. of A. V., R. V., is not here quite exact; v. 1-3 form

---

[2] *Commentaries on the Four Last Books of Moses*, Eng. Tr., Vol. III, p. 94. "Caeterum quidam interpretes non legunt hos tres versus uno contextu, sed plenam sententiam esse volunt, ut maritus testetur se divortium facere cum uxore, non ob crimen, sed quia formae venustas eius libidini non satisfaciat. Si quis tamen propius attendat, facile videbit unum esse duntaxat legis caput, nempe, ubi quis uxorem repudiaverit, fas non esse iterum eam ducere si alteri nupserit" (*Opera*, Brunswick, 1882, Vol. XXIV, p. 658).

[3] *Biblical Commentary on the Old Testament*, Eng. Tr., Edinburgh, 1880. Vol. III, pp. 416 f.

the protasis, stating the conditions of the case contemplated,
v. ⁴ is the apodosis".⁴ To the same effect is the comment of
Joseph Reider: "The chief concern of the law is to prevent
remarriage after divorce. Consequently vv. 1–3 must be
construed as the protasis and v. 4 alone as the apodosis."⁵

To these might be added the same judgment on the part
of others. We can properly regard this view of the construction and intent of the passage as the one in favour of which
there is an overwhelming preponderance. It is surely a consideration weighted with the closest bearing on this question
that the oldest and, on all accounts, the most important
version, the Septuagint, adopts this construction.⁶ As translated the whole passage should then read as follows:

> When a man taketh a wife, and marrieth her, and it cometh
> to pass, if she find no favour in his eyes, because he hath
> found in her some unseemly thing, that he writeth her a
> bill of divorcement, and giveth it into her hand, and
> sendeth her out of his house, and she departeth out of his
> house, and goeth and becometh another man's wife, and
> the latter husband hateth her and writeth her a bill of
> divorcement, and giveth it into her hand, and sendeth her
> out of his house, or if the latter husband, who took her to
> be his wife, die; her former husband, which sent her away,
> may not take her again to be his wife, after that she has
> been defiled, for this is an abomination before the Lord,
> and thou shalt not cause the land to sin which the Lord
> thy God giveth thee for an inheritance.

These observations with respect to construction are of
primary importance because they show that this passage does
not make divorce mandatory in the case of the indecency or
uncleanness concerned. It is not even to be understood as
encouraging or advising men to put away their wives in such
a case. Neither is it to be understood as an authorising or

---

⁴ *The International Critical Commentary, A Critical and Exegetical Commentary on Deuteronomy*, New York, 1916, p. 269.

⁵ *Op. cit.*, p. 220. The Revised Standard Version (1952) adopts this view
of the construction.

⁶ Ἐὰν δέ τις λάβῃ γυναῖκα καὶ συνοικήσῃ αὐτῇ, καὶ ἔσται ἐὰν μὴ
εὕρῃ χάριν ἐναντίον αὐτοῦ ὅτι εὗρεν ἐν αὐτῇ ἄσχημον πρᾶγμα, καὶ
γράψει αὐτῇ βιβλίον ἀποστασίου . . . οὐ δυνήσεται ὁ ἀνὴρ ὁ πρότερος
ὁ ἐξαποστείλας αὐτὴν ἐπαναστέψας λαβεῖν αὐτὴν ἑαυτῷ γυναῖκα μετὰ
τὸ μιανθῆναι αὐτήν . . .

sanctioning of divorce. It simply provides that if a man puts away his wife and she marries another man the former husband cannot under any conditions take her again to be his wife. There is nothing, therefore, in this passage itself to warrant the conclusion that divorce is here given divine approval and is morally legitimated under the conditions specified.[7]

It must, of course, be fully conceded that divorce was practised. This is taken for granted in this passage, so much so that under certain conditions it is permanently valid and inviolable. Other passages in the Pentateuch also evince the practice of divorce (Lev. 21:7, 14; 22:13; Numb. 30:9 (10); Deut. 22:19, 29; cf. Isa. 50:1; Jer. 3:1; Ezek. 44:22).

It is also conceded that divorce was permitted or tolerated. This is true not simply in the sense in which every event that

---

[7] Commentators like Driver and Reider, for example, though insistent that verses 1–3 are protasis and verse 4 alone apodosis, nevertheless assume that the *right* of divorce is taken for granted. The former says: "The law is thus not, properly speaking, a law of divorce: the right of divorce is assumed, as established by custom (comp. 22 [19.29], two cases in which the right is forfeited); but definite legal formalities are prescribed, and restrictions are imposed, tending to prevent its being lightly or rashly exercised" (*op. cit.*, p. 269). Reider likewise says: "Here, as elsewhere (Lev. 21.7, 14; 22.13; Num. 30.10), the right of divorce is taken for granted (it was an absolute right, vested in man, among all Semitic nations), hence there are no regulations concerning it" (*op. cit.*, p. 220). It is this view that is being controverted in this article. To say the least, the writer maintains that to speak of divorce in this connection as a right is not precisely correct. The viewpoint adopted is rather in line with that of Augustine, Calvin, Keil and Delitzsch and others (*cf.*, Calvin: *op. cit.*, pp. 93 f.; Keil and Delitzsch: *op. cit.*, pp. 416 ff.; Rudolf Stier: *The Words of the Lord Jesus*, Eng. Tr., Edinburgh, 1855, Vol. I, p. 175). Augustine's comment is worth quoting here. Referring to the looseness of Gentile practice he says: "Something similar to this custom, on account of the hardness of the Israelites, Moses seems to have allowed, concerning a bill of divorcement (Deut. 24:1; Matt. 19:8). In which matter there appears rather reproof than approval of divorce" (*De Bono Conjugali, Lib.* I, *Cap.* VIII; *cf.* also *Contra Faustum Manichaeum, Lib.* XIX, *Cap.* XXVI).

In fairness to Driver and as more in accord with the position taken above a later comment of his should be quoted. He says: "Hebrew law, as remarked above, does not institute divorce, but tolerates it, in view of the imperfections of human nature (πρὸς τὴν σκληροκαρδίαν ὑμῶν, Matt. 19 [8]), and lays down regulations tending to limit it, and preclude its abuse" (*op. cit.*, p. 272). It may well be that Driver is not using the word "right" in the sense of intrinsic right and prerogative.

occurs is permitted but in the sense that it was conceded or suffered as the actual *status quo*, and the penalty of civil or ecclesiastical ostracism was not attached to it. This is just saying that a certain freedom in the matter of divorce was tolerated and when that freedom was exercised a civil or ecclesiastical penalty was not thereby incurred. Deuteronomy 22:19, 29 instances two cases in which this very freedom was denied and these provisions imply that a certain kind of freedom might be exercised by others who did not fall into either of these two categories. In this respect the difference between the Old and New Testaments appears. As we shall see later on, this freedom, conceded or suffered under the Mosaic economy, is removed under the gospel dispensation.

It is highly necessary, however, to distinguish between this sufferance or toleration, on the one hand, and divine approval or sanction, on the other. As found already there is no evidence to show that divorce was approved or morally legitimated. Permission, sufferance, toleration was granted. But underlying this very notion is the idea of wrong. We do not properly speak of toleration or sufferance as granted or conceded in connection with what is intrinsically right or desirable. It is this line of distinction, too often forgotten or obliterated, that must be appreciated, and it is this distinction that underlies or is expressed in the treatment our Lord provides on this question, as we shall see later.

When we say that an intrinsic wrong is presupposed in the very sufferance accorded, it is not meant simply that a general or specific sinful condition is presupposed in the practice of divorce but also that in the very act of divorce itself there is an intrinsic wrong not compatible with the absolute standard of right. And by sufferance is meant that, while the act was intrinsically wrong and therefore worthy of censure, the sanctions attached to this evil were not as severe as the intrinsic evil of the practice merited. For the hardness of their heart Moses suffered them to put away their wives. The subsequent discussion will show that the restrictions imposed upon the divorce tolerated and practised were necessitated by the very abnormalities and evils associated with the practice.

The Bill of Divorcement. The bill of divorcement (סֵפֶר כְּרִיתֻת),[8] we have good reason to believe, was mandatory in the case of dismissal. It served a variety of purposes. It was a legal document and therefore served as a deterrent of hasty action on the part of the husband — it would serve to restrain frivolous, thoughtless and rash dismissal. It would also be a testimonial to the woman of her freedom from marital obligations to the husband who sent her away. And it would be a protective instrument in the matter of the woman's reputation and well-being, particularly in the event that she married another man.[9]

We may conclude that the bill of divorcement was required by positive enactment in all cases of divorce and was therefore in the category of precept or requirement. This should be borne in mind, as it may bear very closely upon the interpretation of the New Testament passages.

The Unseemly Thing. It has to be admitted that it is exceedingly difficult if not precarious to be certain as to what the "unseemly thing" really was. The Hebrew is עֶרְוַת דָּבָר and literally means "nakedness of a thing". As is well known,

---

[8] An example of the bill of divorce can be seen in John Lightfoot: *Horae Hebraicae et Talmudicae, Works,* ed. Pitman, London, 1823, Vol. XI, p. 120. *Cf.,* however, E. Neufeld: *Ancient Hebrew Marriage Laws,* London, 1944, p. 180. Neufeld says, "the prescribed contents of the letter of divorce are unknown" and contends that "the historical data at hand suggest that there was a short formula".

[9] "The *writing of divorcement,* therefore, was itself no hardship, but a benefit, protecting the divorced wife from unfounded imputations, and declaring her repudiation to be founded upon something less than violation of her marriage vow. This was the requisition of the law; but what was the corruption or the false interpretation of it, tacitly implied and afterwards refuted? This, we learn from a fuller declaration of our Saviour on a different occasion, which has been preserved by Mark (10, 2–12), consisted in regarding the Mosaic precept as a license to repudiate at will; whereas it was a merciful provision in behalf of the repudiated woman, designed to mitigate the hardship of divorces, even when unlawful. It was not a general permission to repudiate, but a stringent requisition that whoever did so should secure his wife from injury by certifying that she was not chargeable with unchaste conduct, but divorced upon some minor pretext" (Joseph Addison Alexander: *The Gospel according to Matthew Explained,* London, 1884, p. 145; *cf.* also Driver: *op. cit.,* pp. 272 f.).

Rabbinical interpretation was sharply divided on this question. The school of Shammai regarded it as unchastity of behaviour, the school of Hillel as any indecency or anything displeasing to the husband. Some of the latter school deemed most frivolous reasons as sufficient.[10]

The divergence in Rabbinical interpretation provides us with a convenient approach to the question. If the interpretation of the former school should be demonstrated to be correct, then the Mosaic legislation here would be almost identical with the provisions of the New Testament on this question.[11] An examination of the evidence will show, however, that the truth does not seem to rest with either of these views.

The following facts bear most cogently against the view that עֶרְוַת דָּבָר refers to adultery.

(1) The Pentateuch prescribed death for adultery (Lev. 20:10; Deut. 22:22; cf. Deut. 22:23–27). It must be concluded, therefore, that the provisions of Deuteronomy 24:1–4 cannot apply to a case of proven adultery on the part of the wife. She and her guilty partner were both put to death.

[10] The Talmudical Tract *Gittin* deals with this diversity of interpretation. As translated by Leo Auerbach it says: "The House of Shamai says: A man must not divorce his wife unless he has found her unfaithful. As was said (Deuteronomy xxiv, 1) *Because he hath found some uncleanness in her.* The House of Hillel says: He may divorce her if she only spoiled a dish for him because it was said: Uncleanness is anything. Rabbi Akiba says: He may divorce her if he found another that is more beautiful than his wife, because it was said: (Deut. xxiv, 1) *If it come to pass that she find no favour in his eyes*" (*The Babylonian Talmud in Selection*, New York, 1944, p. 178; cf. also Lightfoot: *op. cit.*, p. 117).

[11] John Lightfoot regards the עֶרְוַת דָּבָר as meaning adultery. He reconciles this with the other provisions of the Pentateuch regarding adultery by arguing thus: "When God had established that fatal law of punishing adultery by death (Deut. xxii.), for the terror of the people, and for their avoiding of that sin; the same merciful God foreseeing, also, how hard (occasion being taken from this law) the issue of this might be to the women, by reason of the roughness of the men, — lusting, perhaps after other women, and loathing their own wives, — he mere graciously provided against such kind of wife-killing by a law, mitigating the former, and allowed the putting away a wife in the same case, concerning which that fatal law was given, — namely, in the case of adultery" (*op. cit.*, p. 116: see also p. 117).

(2) It might, however, be pleaded that though the divorce legislation could not apply to a case of proven adultery it might apply to a case of adultery not proven but on good grounds suspected. The provisions of Numbers 5:11–31 have to do with such a case and the ritual prescribed leaves no place for divorce. This same passage has to do also with the case of the man who entertains suspicion or jealousy with reference to his wife when there is no ground in fact for such suspicion. The provisions of Deuteronomy 24:1–4 cannot therefore apply to a case of suspected adultery whether such suspicion be warranted or unwarranted.

(3) Furthermore, the Pentateuch deals with the case of a man who brings against his newly-wedded wife the charge of uncleanness (Deut. 22:13–21). If the charge is disproven by the presentation of the tokens of virginity on the part of the father and mother of the damsel, then the man may not put her away — "she shall be his wife; he may not put her away all his days" (vs. 19). If the tokens of virginity were not found in the damsel, she was to be stoned to death. So again the provisions of Deuteronomy 24:1–4 cannot apply to this case.

(4) In Deuteronomy 22:23, 24 we have the provisions for uncleanness on the part of a virgin betrothed unto a husband. In this case both the virgin betrothed and the man who defiled her were to be put to death.

(5) In the case of a betrothed virgin who was forced, Deuteronomy 22:25–27 provides that the man only was to be put to death and the virgin was to be treated as guiltless.

(6) In the case of a man who lies with a virgin not betrothed, the requirement of Deuteronomy 22:28, 29 is that the man must marry the damsel and he may not put her away all his days.

We see then that the law provides for all sorts of contingencies in the matter of sexual uncleanness. But in none of the cases instanced above does the phrase עֶרְוַת דָּבָר or even the word עֶרְוָה occur. In every case the remedy or redress is entirely different from recourse to divorce. In none of these contingencies could the prescriptions of Deuteronomy 24:1–4 apply. We must conclude, therefore, that there is no evidence to show that עֶרְוַת דָּבָר refers to adultery or to an act of sexual uncleanness. Indeed the evidence is preponderantly against any such interpretation.[12]

On the other hand, the looser interpretation of the school of Hillel does not appear to be well supported. The phrase itself when viewed in the context of Old Testament usage surely requires something shameful. While it is true that the phrase עֶרְוַת דָּבָר itself occurs only once elsewhere in the Old Testament (Deut. 23:14 (15)), the word עֶרְוָה occurs frequently in the sense of shameful exposure of the human body (*cf.* Gen. 9:22, 23; Exod. 20:26; Lam. 1:8; Ezek. 16:36, 37). Furthermore, the word is frequently used of illicit sexual intercourse (*cf.* especially Lev. 18), even though, as we found above, there is no evidence to show that the phrase עֶרְוַת דָּבָר means illicit sexual intercourse in Deuteronomy 24:1. And in Deuteronomy 23:14 (15), the only other instance of the phrase in the Old Testament, it is used with reference to the human excrement, and the "unclean thing" is the failure to cover up the human excrement in accordance with the law set forth in the preceding verses. We may conclude that עֶרְוַת דָּבָר means some indecency or impropriety of behaviour; it might be in the category of defect or omission. While falling short of illicit sexual intercourse it may well be that the indecency consisted in some kind of shameful conduct connected with sex life. Or it may have been some other kind of impropriety worthy of censure on the part of the husband.

It is, consequently, necessary to strike a balance between the rigid interpretation of the school of Shammai and the loose one of the school of Hillel. We must suppose something shameful and offensive that gives to the husband some legitimate ground for displeasure and complaint.[13]

---

[12] *Cf.* Keil and Delitzsch: *op. cit.*, p. 417; Driver: *op. cit.*, p. 271; Reider: *op. cit.*, p. 221; Alexander: *op. cit.*, p. 145. Alexander's comment is: "That the bill or writing was not a charge of infidelity, but rather a certificate of innocence in that respect, is clear, because it was to be delivered to the wife herself, and because the law required an adultress to be punished (Num. 5, 31), not to be thus quietly dismissed".

[13] *Cf.*, *e. g.*, Neufeld: *op. cit.*, p. 179. "It would thus seem that the phrase denoted some gross indecency, some singular impropriety, which

The Defilement and Abomination. The reason why the divorced woman who has married another man may not under any circumstances return to her first husband is that by her second marriage she has been defiled (הֻטַּמָּאָה). This root (טָמֵא) is used very frequently in the Old Testament, particularly in the Pentateuch. It is used of moral, religious or ceremonial pollution. The strength and force of the word may be seen by the fact that when used of moral defilement it can refer to the grossest types of sexual immorality and when used of religious defilement can refer to the gross iniquity of idolatry.

An examination of the Old Testament usage will evince that the defilement involved in this case cannot be reduced to the level of merely ceremonial defilement but will have to be placed in the same category as Leviticus 18:20 and Numbers 5:13, 14, 20, 27, 28, 29. There is no ceremonial ritual that can remove the defilement, as in other cases where ceremonial uncleanness is in view. And if the defilement is not taken into account and the prohibition to return to the first husband is violated, the evil is an abomination (תּוֹעֵבָה) to the Lord and it causes the land to sin.

The very nature of the restriction imposed shows that some kind of gross abnormality is regarded as entering into the situation. In normal conditions a woman whose husband died was at liberty to marry another man. If no abnormality entered into this case we should think that it would be most natural and normal for the woman to return to her first husband in the event of the death of her second. But it is just here that the law is most jealous. Even in the case of the death of the second husband the woman may not return to her first husband. The severity of the restriction and the reason assigned show the gross irregularity of the situation created by the second marriage — "she has been defiled".

It should be noted that the divorced woman is not prevented from returning to her husband if she did not marry a second. It is only in the event of remarriage that the defilement enters

aroused the revulsion of the husband and made his life with her henceforth an impossibility."

and the prohibition takes effect. It should also be noted that the law at this point does not prevent a woman from marrying a third husband in the event that the second husband divorces her or dies. But in no case may she return to a former husband if once married to another. This peculiarity is very striking and shows the grave complication that is liable to arise once a bill of divorcement is given. While the bill of divorcement as such does not prevent reconciliation and restoration, yet once a second marriage is consummated the whole relationship changes. The second marriage effects an unobliterable separation from the first husband. This implies a unique relation to the first husband and demonstrates that the marriage bond is so sacred that, although divorce may be given and a certain freedom granted to the divorced persons, yet there is an unobliterable relationship that appears, paradoxically enough, in the form of an unobliterable separation in the event that a second marriage has been consummated on the part of the divorced wife. This irremediable separation only serves to enforce the gross abnormality entailed and serves to confirm the interpretation given earlier as to the import of this passage. Divorce was not required, legitimated, sanctioned or encouraged. It was rather discouraged, and the severity of the restriction imposed, together with the reason assigned for this restriction, enforces that discouragement. Divorce was indeed tolerated or suffered. But the evil and wrong presupposed in that very sufferance receive emphatic declaration in the provision of Deuteronomy 24:4. The penal sanction attached is a witness to the unobliterable irregularity entailed in the divorce.

It should indeed be noted that it is only with reference to the prohibited return to the first husband that the defilement concerned is mentioned. The remarriage on the part of the divorced woman is not expressly stated to be defilement irrespective of return to the first husband. For these considerations we are required to exercise great caution before stigmatising the remarriage as adulterous. One thing is certain, that the second marriage was not placed in the category of adultery nor the woman regarded as an adulteress in terms of the Pentateuchal legislation. The woman and her second husband were not put to death as the Pentateuch required in the case of adultery. While not stigmatised as adultery in terms of the Mosaic economy, nevertheless, it is not at all so certain that the remarriage is not regarded as involving defilement. It may very well be that the evil attaching to divorce and the abnormal situation in which the woman is placed as the divorcee of her first husband are regarded as casting their shadow over the second marriage even though the second marriage is not placed in the category of adultery and civil or ecclesiastical penalty is not appended.

But even if we suppose that defilement is not regarded as inhering in the second marriage *per se*, we must observe that the moment return to the first husband is envisaged, then the marital relation to the second husband takes on an entirely different complexion. Whatever may be true of the second marriage, irrespective of return to the first husband, the moment return is envisaged, then, with reference to the first husband, the woman has been defiled. And it is this restoration that is called an abomination. All of this forcibly reminds us of the grave abnormalities that inhere in the practice of divorce. The one insurmountable obstacle to the marriage of this particular woman with this particular man is not that the woman had been married to another man but simply that the particular man concerned is the man from whom she had been divorced. It is the fact of divorce that bears the whole onus of ultimate responsibility for the defilement that is sure to enter when the first marriage is restored after a second had been consummated.

Conclusion. Thus within the limits of this passage we have exemplified and confirmed the principle that while divorce was suffered in the Mosaic economy we have no warrant to suppose that under any circumstances was it sanctioned or approved as the intrinsic right or prerogative of the husband. It should not be claimed that this interpretation resolves all difficulties connected with the practice of divorce. But it is a construction of the passage that is grammatically, syntactically, and exegetically defensible and it brings principial harmony into the teaching of the Old Testament. It eliminates the inconsistency that inheres in the very notion of approval or sanction and it accords to the practice of divorce a status

that is principially consistent with the original institution of
Genesis 2:23, 24 and in harmony with the final word of the
Old Testament on this question:

> And this have ye done again, covering the altar of the
> Lord with tears, with weeping, and with crying out, inso-
> much that he regardeth not the offering any more, or
> receiveth *it* with good will at your hand.
> Yet ye say, Wherefore? Because the Lord hath been
> witness between thee and the wife of thy youth, against
> whom thou hast dealt treacherously: yet *is* she thy com-
> panion, and the wife of thy covenant.
> And did not he make one? Yet had he the residue of the
> spirit. And wherefore one? That he might seek a godly
> seed. Therefore take heed to your spirit, and let none
> deal treacherously against the wife of his youth.
> For the Lord, the God of Israel, saith that he hateth
> putting away: for *one* covereth violence with his garment,
> saith the Lord of hosts: therefore take heed to your spirit.
> that ye deal not treacherously (Malachi 2:13–16).

II

The Teaching of Our Lord

Matthew 5:31, 32

This is the first passage in the New Testament that deals with the question of divorce. Since it occurs in the discourse of our Lord known as the sermon on the mount, it is necessary at the outset to make a few observations bearing upon the formula used repeatedly in this part of the discourse and appearing in the passage with which we are directly concerned. The formula to which we refer is: "it was said . . . but I say to you" (ἐρρέθη . . . ἐγὼ δὲ λέγω ὑμῖν). It occurs in this chapter on six occasions — 5:21, 22; 5:27, 28; 5:31, 32; 5:33, 34; 5:38, 39; 5:43, 44. The contrast implicit in this formula is not to be interpreted as if our Lord were placing his own legislative teaching in opposition to the law of the Old Testament; far less is it to be regarded as implying abrogation of the Old Testament law. This should be obvious particularly for two reasons.

(a) In his introduction to the part of the discourse that is built around the repeated use of this formula Jesus emphatically disavows that he came to destroy the law (vss. 17–20). "Think not that I came to destroy the law or the prophets: I came not to destroy but to fulfil" (vs. 17). The verb used here, translated "destroy", is one that might properly be rendered "abrogate". He came not to abrogate but to fulfil. In the succeeding verse he provides the reason in the language of emphatic asseveration: "For verily I say to you, until heaven and earth pass away, one jot or one tittle shall by no means pass from the law, till all be fulfilled" (vs. 18). The two remaining verses (19, 20) offer the strongest confirmation of Jesus' denial that he had come to abro-

gate — they affirm the seriousness of the consequences entailed in the breach and disparagement of even the least of
the commandments of the law. In verse 19 Jesus indicates
that one's relative position in the kingdom of heaven is
determined by his practical conduct and didactic activity
in reference to the least of the commandments. In verse 20
he institutes a principle of exclusion from the kingdom of
heaven, a principle of righteousness that is to be measured
by the norm of the divine law. It is quite impossible, therefore, to interpret this jealousy for the minutiae of the Old
Testament law as compatible with the notion of abrogation.
Jesus came not to break down but to bring to completion
and fulfilment.

(b) In developing the thought introduced by the formula,
it is made abundantly plain in particular cases that Jesus
cannot be relaxing the obligation of the commandment to
which he makes allusion. He is showing rather the breadth
and depth of its application. This appears most conspicuously
in the sections which deal with the sixth and seventh commandments (vss. 21–26 and 27–32 respectively). In the
former Jesus is showing that the commandment, "Thou shalt
not kill" has reference not simply to the external act of murder
but to the very feeling of unholy anger and to the words of
abusive contempt. In the latter he is showing that the commandment, "Thou shalt not commit adultery" has reference
to the lascivious thought and desire of the heart as well as to
the overt act of uncleanness. It is impossible to think of
Jesus as abrogating the commandment in either case. That
with which his own solemn asseveration is concerned and
that upon which he pronounces the severest judgment is the
murder and adultery of the heart. How then could he in the
least degree be abrogating the commandments which prohibit the very vices he condemns? He is rather confirming
the sanctity of these commands and in so doing lays bare the
spirituality of their obligation and application.

The contrast instituted in the formula, therefore, cannot
be a contrast between the legislation of the Old Testament
and the legislation Jesus himself is inaugurating. The import
of the formula must be sought in some other direction. It is
beyond the scope of this article to demonstrate by detailed

examination of all the passages what the intent of our Lord was.[1] But it could readily be shown that what Jesus is contrasting is not his own law and the law of the Old Testament but rather the true import and intent of the Old Testament law as authoritatively interpreted by himself, on the one hand, and the perversions and distortions to which that law had been subjected by pharisaical and rabbinical externalism, on the other. This is the principle that will be found to apply in every case in which the formula occurs.

It must not be supposed, however, that the denial of antithesis between the Old Testament law and the law Jesus himself enunciates in any way eliminates the original divine authority with which Jesus spoke. The asseveration, "But I say to you" is itself redolent of an authority that is divine. It is not without purpose that Matthew, when he resumes his narrative after the sermon on the mount, continues, "And it came to pass when Jesus had finished these sayings, the people were astonished at his teaching: for he was teaching them as having authority, and not as their scribes" (Matt. 7:28, 29). Jesus is inaugurating the kingdom of heaven. The circumstances of the sermon on the mount were indeed very different from those which Israel witnessed at Sinai. Yet in Jesus' words we can hear the thunder of the divine voice. And it is a divine voice that promulgates law with seals and sanctions no less authenticative than those of Sinai. It is this divine authority with which Jesus speaks that must be borne in mind when, later on, we discover an enactment which must be interpreted as amendment and abolition of certain temporary Mosaic provisions.

When we turn to Matthew 5:31, 32, we cannot mistake the express allusion to the Old Testament provision governing divorce in Deuteronomy 24:1–4. "It was said, whosoever shall put away his wife, let him give her a bill of divorce" (ἀποστάσιον). It is apparent that the primary, if not exclusive, reference is to Deuteronomy 24:1 While this is undoubtedly the case, nevertheless two features of this passage in Matthew 5:31 must be noted.

---

[1] For a fuller discussion of the antitheses see Ned Bernard Stonehouse: *The Witness of Matthew and Mark to Christ*, pp. 197–211.

(1) The form in which the allusion to Deuteronomy 24:1 appears is not a verbatim quotation either from the Hebrew text or from the Septuagint version of the passage. While it is true that the bill of divorcement was required in every case of divorce, as we found in the preceding chapter in this volume, and while the form used here by Christ may simply focus attention upon that fact and be therefore a perfectly proper paraphrase of this provision implied in Deuteronomy 24:1, yet it is also true that the form used by our Lord may reflect a distorted version of the Deuteronomic provision, a distortion current in Judaism, which Jesus proceeds to correct.

(2) More particularly must it be noted that the form used here by our Lord does not imply that Deuteronomy 24:1 gave to the Israelites the right to put away their wives; far less does it imply that in certain cases the Israelites were under obligation to put away their wives. The language used cannot strictly be interpreted to imply any more than that, if a man did put away his wife, it was necessary for him to give her a bill of divorcement. In other words, the form used implies that provision was made for a certain contingency but does not determine whether the contingency itself was right or wrong. This text, therefore, does not in the least interfere with the interpretation of Deuteronomy 24:1–4 presented in the preceding chapter.

In verse 32 Jesus proceeds to propound the principle that to put away or dismiss a wife for any reason but that of sexual infidelity is sin. Before undertaking to discuss the express teaching of this text it is well to bear in mind that there are two subjects closely germane to this whole question of divorce on which this text does not reflect. First, the text deals exclusively with dismissal or divorce on the part of the man; what rights may belong to the woman in the matter of suing out a divorce are not intimated. Secondly, Jesus says nothing here with respect to the question of the remarriage of the man who puts away his wife for the cause of fornication.

The express teaching of the text may be set forth under the following subdivisions.

(i) Fornication is unequivocally stated to be the only legitimate ground for which a man may put away his wife. The

word used here is the more generic term for sexual unclean-
ness, namely, fornication ($\pi o \rho \nu \epsilon i a$). This term may be used
of all kinds of illicit sexual intercourse and may apply to such
on the part of unmarried persons, in whose case the sin would
not be in the specific sense adultery. But though it is the
generic word that is used here (*cf.* also Matt. 19:9), it is not
to be supposed that the sense is perplexed thereby. What
Jesus sets in the forefront is the sin of illicit sexual intercourse. It is, of course, implied that such on the part of a
married woman is not only fornication but also adultery in
the specific sense, for the simple reason that it constitutes
sexual infidelity to her spouse. And this is the only case in
which, according to Christ's unambiguous assertion, a man
may dismiss his wife without being involved in the sin which
Jesus proceeds to characterise as making his wife to be an
adulteress.

It should be observed that Jesus does not say that the
husband in such a case is obliged to put away his wife. Whatever may be the truth respecting this question it is not ani-
madverted upon in this text. All that is stated is that if the
husband puts away for this reason he is not involved in the
sin specified.

What is of paramount importance is that however significant is the exceptive clause as guarding the innocence of the
husband in dismissing for sexual infidelity, it is not the exceptive clause that bears the weight of the emphasis in the text.
It is rather that the husband may not put away *for any other
cause*. It is the *one* exception that gives prominence to the
illegitimacy of any other reason. Preoccupation with the one
exception should never be permitted to obscure the force of
the negation of all others.

(ii) The evil of putting away (for any other reason than
that of adultery) is viewed from the standpoint of what it
entails for the woman divorced. The man "makes her to
be an adulteress" ($\pi o \iota \epsilon \hat{\iota} \; a \dot{v} \tau \grave{\eta} \nu \; \mu o \iota \chi \epsilon v \theta \hat{\eta} \nu a \iota$). If we are to
give passive force to the infinitive in this clause, it could be
rendered, "he makes her to suffer adultery".[2] The man is

---

[2] The passive of the verb $\mu o \iota \chi \epsilon \acute{v} \omega$ occurs very infrequently in Biblical
Greek. In addition to this verse the only instances in the New Testament

not said in this case to commit adultery; his sin is rather
that he becomes implicated in the wrong of adultery on the
part of his dismissed wife.

are Matthew 19:9 and John 8:4. This reading in Matthew 19:9 is not to
be adopted as the genuine text even though attested by Codex Vaticanus
and some cursives. But in any case it adds nothing to the clarification of
the meaning because it is exactly parallel to Matthew 5:32 and the context affords no additional light. Apart altogether from the textual question, John 8:4 is helpful in determining the meaning of the passive, if
μοιχευομένη is regarded as passive rather than middle.

In the Septuagint a possible instance of the passive of μοιχεύω occurs
apparently in only one instance in the canonical books, namely, Leviticus 20:10. It occurs also in the apocryphal book Sirach 23:23. Leviticus
20:10 is as follows: ἄνθρωπος, ὃς ἂν μοιχεύσηται γυναῖκα ἀνδρὸς ἢ
ὃς ἂν μοιχεύσηται γυναῖκα τοῦ πλησίον, θανάτῳ θανατούσθωσαν ὁ
μοιχεύων καὶ ἡ μοιχευομένη.

μοιχεύσηται in both cases is aorist subjunctive middle and renders the
imperfect Qal of the Hebrew verb נאף. It is apparent that the sense is
active and means, "to commit adultery", as does the Hebrew יִנְאַף. ἡ
μοιχευομένη translates the Hebrew active participle הַנֹּאָפֶת and means
"the adulteress", corresponding to ὁ μοιχεύων which translates the Hebrew active participle הַנֹּאֵף and means "the adulterer". We must, of
course, reckon with the fact that μοιχευομένη may be a present middle
participle. The form would be the same in both middle and passive. But,
if it is passive, this is a case where a passive of μοιχεύω bears distinctly
active meaning. It is indeed abstractly conceivable that the passive form
bears something of the passive meaning and in that case could be rendered,
"the woman made to suffer adultery". It may be that in the act of adultery
the woman is considered as more passive than the man. Two observations, however, must be made. First, there is nothing in the context, or
in the Hebrew that lies back of the Greek, to suggest any such passive
force. Secondly, the woman in this case is treated with the same degree
of severity as the man. She bears the penalty of death as the man does.
If she were regarded as less guilty we might expect some kind of ameliora-
tion in the penalty executed. And if she were the helpless victim of the
adulterer's lust, we may be sure that more merciful provisions would have
been enacted, as in the case of Deuteronomy 22:25–27.

Sirach 23:23 is particularly interesting. The preceding context deals
with the punishment that is meted out to the fornicator. The more immediate context characterises the sin and retribution of "the wife who
leaves her husband and brings in an heir by a stranger" (vs. 22). Verse 23
catalogues her sins. It is here that the aorist passive of μοιχεύω occurs —
καὶ τὸ τρίτον ἐν πορνείᾳ ἐμοιχεύθη καὶ ἐξ ἀλλοτρίου ἀνδρὸς τέκνα
παρέστησεν. It is possible that this might be rendered, "And, thirdly,
she is made to suffer adultery in fornication and bringeth in children by
a strange man". The force of the passive would thus be retained. The

Admittedly this phrase, "to suffer adultery"! is a difficult one. It should be apparent that the wife does not become

more natural rendering, however, would be, "she committeth adultery in fornication and bringeth in children by a strange man". But, in any case, active wrongdoing on the part of the woman is contemplated in the use of the aorist passive. She is not simply a woman who has been wronged by the aggressive assault of a man; far less is she a woman who has been simply "stigmatised as adulterous". She is the woman "who leaves her husband", "who is disobedient to the law of the Most High" and "trespasses against her own husband". Without question, ἐμοιχεύθη here denotes the most notorious kind of adulterous behaviour on the part of the woman.

In John 8:4 we have another instance of the participle μοιχευομένη which may be either passive or middle. The most natural rendering is that of "committing adultery". It is possible that the passive meaning, "being debauched" or "being caused to suffer adultery" appears. But in view of the occurrence in verse 3 of the phrase, ἐν μοιχείᾳ κατειλημμένην it is far more natural to take μοιχευομένη in verse 4 in the active sense of committing adultery — "this woman was taken in the very act, committing adultery". In any case, even if it were regarded as passive rather than middle there is no warrant to suppose that the woman was not regarded as involved in the sin of adultery. On the contrary, she was regarded as one guilty of the sin for which Moses prescribed death by stoning (vs. 5; cf. vs. 11).

In Matthew 5:32, therefore, it is not impossible to regard μοιχευθῆναι as having an active meaning, namely, to "commit adultery". In this case the clause would be rendered, "he makes her to commit adultery". But whether this be the sense or not, it is not feasible to exclude from the word μοιχευθῆναι actual involvement in the sin of adultery. Let the sense be active or passive, the woman is conceived of as entering into adulterous relations.

μοιχᾶται is present indicative middle. Any attempt to remove from the word the notion of active participation in the sin of adultery is entirely indefensible. Cf. Matthew 19:9; Mark 10:11; Jeremiah 3:8; 5:7; 7:9; 9:1; 23:14.

R. C. H. Lenski (*Interpretation of St. Matthew's Gospel*, Columbus, 1932, pp. 226 ff.) insists upon the passive force of μοιχευθῆναι and μοιχᾶται in this verse and strenuously controverts the rendering " 'to commit adultery' (active)" in both cases. In order "to bring out the passive sense of the Greek forms" he adopts the rendering "stigmatised as adulterous" for both forms. He contends that "all that the passive μοιχευθῆναι states is that the woman has been forced into a position that looks to men as if she too had violated the Commandment οὐ μοιχεύσεις ... Her wicked husband has fastened this stigma upon her." He argues that the woman in such a case is not prohibited from marrying again, even though, in doing so, she and her new spouse will be stigmatised as adulterous. Yet an adulteress simply by being divorced. She is contemplated as illegitimately divorced on the part of her wanton husband. She is the victim of his unlawful action, and her station could not therefore in justice be viewed as one of adultery. Indeed, she is viewed as innocent of adultery in the act of divorce and so the act of divorce of which she is not the agent cannot of itself make her an adulteress.

It is necessary, therefore, to envisage some subsequent action in which the woman is involved as drawn within the scope of this expression, "makes her to suffer adultery". Our Lord is no doubt regarding the woman from the station or position in which she is placed by the divorce. She is placed in the position either of being tempted to be joined to another man or being plied with solicitations to union on the part of another man, or indeed, of both. Our Lord is fully cognisant of the weakness of human nature and of the great liability to another marital undertaking on the part of the divorced woman. When that marriage is undertaken, then adultery is committed on the part of that woman and her new consort. This is the significant implication of Jesus' statement. The woman has now become an adulteress and her new spouse an adulterer. This is the entail of moral tragedy that our Lord envisions. And what he says of the husband who divorced the woman is that he is sinfully involved in this moral tragedy. Truly the divorcing husband is not charged with being an adulterer. He is not envisaged as having married again. But he cannot extricate himself from a wrong that involves express adultery on the part of others. It is upon this sin on the part of the divorcing husband that the stress is laid. The sin of remarriage on the part of the

neither of them commits adultery; "they have had something committed upon them".

Such an interpretation of the force of the aorist passive is wholly unwarranted. While it is true that some kind of passive force may have to be recognised, the passive cannot be forced into this kind of service. The idea of merely subjective judgment on the part of others is not inherent in the passive. And whatever strength may be given to the passive in this case, the woman is still viewed as implicated in adultery. There is even less warrant for Lenski's interpretation as it applies to the present indicative middle, μοιχᾶται.

divorced woman is not by any means minimised — she has committed adultery by that remarriage. And it is the sin of adultery that Jesus is condemning in the whole of this sub-section of his discourse. Yet with a finesse of moral judgment that drips with equity the leading thought of the passage focuses attention upon the sin of the divorcing husband — "he makes her to suffer adultery". The moral lessons and the practical implications are too obvious to need comment.

(iii) The remarriage of the woman divorced is adultery on her part and on the part of the man who is joined with her in marriage — "and whosoever marries her who has been put away, commits adultery". The only reason for which this remarriage can be regarded as adulterous is that the first marriage is still in God's sight regarded as inviolate. The divorce has not dissolved it. Illegitimate divorce does not dissolve the marriage bond and consequently the fact of such divorce does not relieve the parties concerned from any of the obligations incident to marriage. They are still in reality bound to one another in the bonds of matrimony and a marital relation or any exercise of the privileges and rights of the marital relation with any other is adultery. Whatever the law of men may enact, this is the law of Christ's kingdom and to it the laws of men should conform.

(iv) It follows from what has been said that the man who divorces his wife (except for the cause of fornication) is not thereby at liberty to remarry any more than the divorced wife. If the woman commits adultery by remarriage, this is so because she is still in reality the wife of the divorcing hus-band. And if so, the divorcing husband is still in reality the husband of the divorced woman and consequently may not marry another. The question as to whether or not the divorc-ing husband may remarry in the event of remarriage on the part of the divorced wife is not reflected upon in this text. This is a perplexing question but need not be discussed now. The question of remarriage on the part of the divorcing hus-band is not introduced in this text except that the remarriage dealt with in the earlier part of this paragraph is excluded by the clear implications just mentioned.

There is, however, another question directly germane to
this text, particularly to the last clause, that requires some
discussion. It is whether the last clause of verse 32 applies
to the remarriage of the woman who has been divorced for
adultery as well as to the remarriage of the woman divorced
without a legitimate reason. As the clause stands by itself
it can well apply to the case of every divorced woman whether
divorced without proper cause or divorced for adultery —
"whosoever marries her who has been put away, commits
adultery". There appear, however, to be good reasons for
thinking that the woman who has been put away (ἀπολελυμένην) is viewed here simply as the woman divorced without
legitimate cause. What bears the burden of emphasis in this
verse is the wrong entailed and the consequences involved
in divorce apart from adultery. The exceptive clause which
prescribes the only legitimate ground of divorce is more or less
parenthetical and should not therefore be erected to a position that disturbs the main thought of the verse. In accordance with this consideration the comment of H. A. W. Meyer
appears to be correct: "That by ἀπολελυμένην, a woman
who is dismissed *illegally*, consequently *not on account of
adultery*, is intended, was understood as a matter of course,
according to the first half of the verse" (Com. *in loc.*).

This, however, does not settle the question as to the status
of the remarriage of the woman divorced for adultery. The
matter is simply left undetermined in the teaching of this
text. The possibility, however, is left open that the force of
the exceptive clause carries over to the last clause of the
verse and, therefore, dissociates the remarriage of the legitimately divorced woman from the adultery contemplated in
the concluding clause, though not, of course, relieving the
woman in any way from the adultery for which she had been
divorced.

In concluding our discussion of this passage it is necessary
to return to the question of the relation of the law enunciated
here by Jesus to the Old Testament law and provisions anent
divorce. The essence of Jesus' teaching in this place is that
there is only one legitimate ground of divorce on the part of
a man and that divorce for any other reason is overt sin and
to be treated accordingly both in our moral judgment and in

jurisprudence. There are certain inferences that call for consideration.

1. We found earlier, in the preceding chapter, that the Old Testament law did not provide for divorce in the case of adultery. The law was more stringent; it required death for such sexual infidelity. The marriage was indeed thereby dissolved but this was effected through the death of the guilty party. The law enunciated by our Lord, on the other hand, institutes divorce as the means of relief for the husband in the case of adultery on the part of his wife. Here then is something novel and it implies that the requirement of death for adultery is abrogated in the economy Jesus himself inaugurated. There are accordingly two provisions which our Lord instituted, one negative and the other positive. He abrogated the Mosaic *penalty* for adultery and he legitimated divorce for adultery. In this very distinctly appears that original legislative authority that pertained to our Lord and it is perhaps the most conspicuous concrete instance of the exercise of that authority in the sermon on the mount.

2. Again we found that the Old Testament did not legitimate, authorise, or sanction divorce for other reasons than that of adultery. In the Mosaic economy, indeed, divorce for the reason mentioned in Deuteronomy 24:1-4 was suffered or tolerated. It was afforded sufferance as an evil, and, because tolerated in practice, was not penalised by civil ostracism or ecclesiastical excommunication in the Mosaic jurisprudence. But the law that Jesus enunciates or institutes is one that obliterates this kind of sufferance or tolerance. In his kingdom the jurisprudence respecting divorce is to be more stringent. The economy he inaugurates is not to be characterised by the laxity inherent in the sufferance afforded in the Mosaic economy. And this means that the reasons given for divorce in Deuteronomy 24:1-4, tolerated in the Mosaic jurisprudence, are abrogated in the New Testament. We have here a striking combination of elements. On the one hand, the abrogation of the death-penalty for adultery and the substitution of divorce as the legitimate resort for the innocent husband indicate a relaxative amendment of the penal sanction attached to adultery. On the other hand,

in the abrogation of the Mosaic sufferance respecting divorce we find an increased severity of moral judgment and legal enactment. The divorce tolerated by Moses is completely reversed and so the very evil recognised and presupposed in the Mosaic sufferance now receives condemnation and correction commensurate with its real character. The right violated in that evil receives its vindication and that principle of right is carried to its logical issue in the prohibition of all such divorce as was suffered under Moses.

It is precisely here that the original and basic law of the Old Testament receives its confirmation, the law presupposed in the very sufferance granted by Moses and the law, as we shall see later, to which Jesus makes his appeal. Our Lord truly abrogates the observance of certain temporary regulations governing the penalty for adultery and he abrogates certain permissions respecting divorce. He did this in the exercise of the legislative authority with which he was invested. But lest we should think that these amendments make less stringent the laws of purity and of the sanctity of the marriage bond, lest we should suppose that Jesus entertains a lower estimate of the binding character of the law of God, we are compelled to perceive that in the abrogation of the divorce tolerated under Moses there is applied a stringency that raises jurisprudence to the level of the intrinsic requirements of the law of God. In doing so Jesus seals and puts into operation the basic and primary principle of the Old Testament law and exemplifies in concrete manner his own protestation, "Think not that I came to destroy the law or the prophets: I came not to destroy, but to fulfil". It is in him and in the economy he establishes that the law receives its completory validation, vindication, application, fulfilment, and embodiment. Could anything be more declarative of the exacting demands of purity and fidelity in the law that regulates Christ's kingdom than the abrogation of every concession to the hardness of men's hearts? This is the force of the pronouncement, "But I say to you that every one who puts away his wife except for fornication makes her to be an adulteress, and whosoever marries her who has been put away, commits adultery".

Matthew 19:3–8

In this passage our Lord's utterances respecting divorce were evoked by the direct question on the part of Pharisees, "Is it lawful for a man to put away his wife for every cause?" This question was doubtless intended to ensnare Jesus and place him under the necessity of taking sides on the question that divided rabbinical interpretation. Our Lord's answer is characteristic. He immediately appeals to Scripture and to the original constitution of the race as male and female. Marriage is grounded in this male and female constitution; as to its nature it implies that the man and woman are united in one flesh; as to its sanction it is divine; and as to its continuance it is permanent. The import of all this is that marriage from its very nature and from the divine institution by which it is constituted is ideally indissoluble. It is not a contract of temporary convenience and not a union that may be dissolved at will.

Jesus skilfully parried the ensnaring question, confronted the Pharisees with first principles and brought them face to face with the sinful conditions under which alone the question of divorce could arise. He enunciated the principles in the light of which the practice of divorce is to be evaluated and its propriety or impropriety determined. Jesus' answer, however, provoked another question on the part of the Pharisees. It is with this question and the answer that we are now mainly concerned.

The question was: "Why then did Moses command to give a bill of divorce and to put away?" The Pharisees must have been alluding to Deuteronomy 24:1–4. It is quite probable that the Pharisees had an erroneous conception of the Deuteronomic passage. In any case it was a garbled version of the passage that was presented in their question. Whether they intentionally garbled the passage or construed it erroneously, they intended, no doubt, to refute or ensnare Jesus by the form of the question.[3]

---

[3] In verse 3 we are told that they came to him tempting him; *cf.* also Mark 10:3.

It is, of course, true that the bill of divorce was mandatory in every case of actual divorce. In that sense it might properly be said that Moses commanded the bill of divorce. There is an element of truth, therefore, in the form of the question. But it can hardly be supposed that it was with this merely contingent requirement that the Pharisees intended to baffle Jesus. To say the least, the question would have been phrased most awkwardly if all they meant by alleging a command on the part of Moses was simply the contingent requirement. Furthermore, their question must in some way be regarded as intimating an antithesis between the alleged command of Moses and the position that had just been enunciated by Jesus himself. The most reasonable interpretation of their question is then that they regarded or at least represented Moses as requiring men to divorce their wives in certain cases. The question with which Jesus would have been confronted, therefore, was one that rested on the assumption that Moses commanded divorce and, in effect, would be as follows: if marriage is really indissoluble according to the original institution, if it is a union that man may not dissolve, how is it that Moses commands divorce? Is there not an antithesis between Jesus' assertions and Moses' commandment? It is this question that Jesus proceeds to answer and his answer is of paramount significance in connection with the whole question of the Mosaic provisions and of the Old Testament law. "He says to them, Moses for the hardness of your heart permitted you to put away your wives: but from the beginning it was not so."

The apparent discrepancy between Matthew 19:7, 8 and Mark 10:3, 4 will be discussed in a subsequent section. It may be said, however, at this point that the question of the Pharisees in Matthew 19:7 might possibly be interpreted in a somewhat weaker sense than that presented above. This weaker sense would suppose that the Pharisees did not intend to represent Moses as positively commanding divorce in certain cases but that they rather wished to represent the Mosaic permission of divorce and the contingent requirement respecting the bill of divorce as constituting a legislative, regulatory enactment on the part of Moses that could not be harmonised with Jesus' assertions regarding the basis and nature of marriage. If this view of the purport of their question were adopted, the antithesis between Jesus' reply and the implications of the Pharisees' question would not be as sharp as that supposed in the argument given above.

What must be appreciated, however, is that even granting this to be the intent of the Pharisees' question the significance of the terms used by Jesus is not thereby eliminated. Whatever may have been the precise import of the Pharisees' question they at least posed the question of the nature and meaning of the Mosaic provisions and the reply of Jesus loses nothing of its significance in the interpretation of the precise nature and character of the Mosaic enactment. The force of the term, "Moses permitted" is not negated by difference of interpretation of the precise import of the Pharisees' question.

The first feature of Jesus' reply that calls for comment is the phrase, "for the hardness of your heart" ($\pi\rho\grave{o}s$ $\tau\grave{\eta}\nu$ $\sigma\kappa\lambda\eta\rho o\kappa\alpha\rho\delta\acute{\iota}\alpha\nu$ $\acute{\upsilon}\mu\hat{\omega}\nu$). It means "in reference to" or "out of regard to" the hardness of your heart and implies that the situation in reference to which or out of consideration for which the Mosaic permission was granted was one created by the stubbornness of the Israelites. The situation that provided occasion for the permission was one of moral perversity and obliquity; it arose from insubordination to and rebellion against the will of God. The implications are very important. For, is it not apparent that the judgment respecting perversity presupposes some law or obligation that is violated or desecrated? Where no law is there is no transgression. The only law or standard relevant to this particular case is that expressed in Genesis 1:27; 2:24. The very judgment respecting hardheartedness, then, presupposes the abiding validity and obligation of the original institution as expounded by Jesus in his answer to the first question of the Pharisees. The original institution and its binding authority had not been abrogated or even suspended, and the moral obliquity of the Israelites consisted in their disposition and determination not to abide by these ordinances. The bill of divorce was directed to this perverse situation and not to the abrogation of the divine institution.

The second element of Jesus' reply concerns the *permission* asserted to have been given by Moses: he "permitted you to put away your wives" (ἐπέτρεψεν ὑμῖν ἀπολῦσαι τὰς γυναῖκας ὑμῶν). The distinction between the verb used by Jesus to denote Moses' action and the verb used by the Pharisees should be carefully noted. The Pharisees alleged that Moses commanded (ἐνετείλατο). Jesus says, Moses permitted (ἐπέτρεψεν). Jesus does not admit or endorse any insinuation or allegation to the effect that Moses commanded divorce. He rather affirms what is of entirely different effect in the interpretation of the Mosaic provisions and particularly of Deuteronomy 24:1–4. The word that Jesus uses is one that implies sufferance or tolerance but in no way implies approval or sanction of the practice, far less authorisation or commandment of it. The Mosaic action is, therefore, two removes from the notion of commandment.

This interpretation on the part of our Lord is wholly in line with, and indeed confirmatory of, the interpretation of Deuteronomy 24:1–4 given in the chapter dealing with that subject. The clear import of Jesus' words is that divorce was suffered in the Mosaic economy because of the hardheartedness of the Israelites. It was a concession to their weakness but did not condone the practice. It was in reality a witness to the gross evil that arose from, or even consisted in, desecration of the divine ordinance, "what therefore God hath joined together, let not man put asunder".

The third feature of our Lord's answer is the contrast he institutes between the permission of Moses and the creation ordinance — "but from the beginning it was not so" (ἀπ' ἀρχῆς δὲ οὐ γέγονεν οὕτως). From the beginning there was no such *permission*. It is not simply that the practice was not commanded, not simply that it was not authorised, not simply that it was not approved, but rather that it was not even *permitted*. The Mosaic permission was, therefore, a departure from the creation ordinance and from the practice to which it obligated men.

In this connection it is well to observe the force of the imperative in verse 6, "let not man put asunder" (ἄνθρωπος μὴ χωριζέτω). In Meyer's words, "Having regard, therefore, to the specific nature of marriage, Jesus utterly condemns divorce generally as being a putting asunder on the part of

man of what, in a very special way, God has joined together"
(*ad loc.*). Divorce is contrary to the divine institution, contrary to the nature of marriage, and contrary to the divine
action by which the union is effected. It is precisely here
that its wickedness becomes singularly apparent — it is the
sundering by man of a union God has constituted. Divorce
is the breaking of a seal which has been engraven by the hand
of God.

Matthew 19:9

As respecting divorce and its implications this is on all
accounts the most pivotal passage in the New Testament.
It occupies this crucial position particularly for the reason
that it is the only passage in the New Testament in which
we have the combination of two clauses, namely, the ex-
ceptive clause ($\mu\dot{\eta} \ \dot{\epsilon}\pi\dot{\iota} \ \pi o\rho\nu\epsilon\dot{\iota}\alpha$) and the remarriage clause
($\kappa\alpha\dot{\iota} \ \gamma\alpha\mu\dot{\eta}\sigma\eta \ \ddot{\alpha}\lambda\lambda\eta\nu$). Both of these clauses occur elsewhere,
the former in Matthew 5:32, in the form $\pi\alpha\rho\epsilon\kappa\tau\dot{o}s \ \lambda\dot{o}\gamma ov$
$\pi o\rho\nu\epsilon\dot{\iota}\alpha s$ and the latter in Mark 10:11, as also in the form
$\kappa\alpha\dot{\iota} \ \gamma\alpha\mu\hat{\omega}\nu \ \dot{\epsilon}\tau\dot{\epsilon}\rho\alpha\nu$ in Luke 16:18. But only in Matthew 19:9
are they coordinated.

It might not be proper to maintain that the question of
the legitimacy of remarriage on the part of the innocent
spouse after divorce for adultery would not arise if we did not
have Matthew 19:9. The question might well emerge in connection with Matthew 5:32. For if a man may rightly divorce
his unfaithful wife and if such divorce dissolves the marriage
bond the question of remarriage is inevitably posed. And,
again, though there is no allusion to adultery as an exception
in Mark 10:11 and Luke 16:18, yet the Old Testament law
respecting adultery and the peculiar character of the sin of
adultery might well compel us to inquire whether or not,
after all, adultery might not have been assumed as a notable
exception to the principle affirmed in these two passages.
Furthermore, I Corinthians 7:15 would certainly face us with
the question of the effect that desertion by an unbelieving
partner would have upon the marital status of the deserted
believer.

Nevertheless, Matthew 19:9 is distinctive in that here the question of the legitimacy or illegitimacy of remarriage after divorce for adultery is thrust upon us directly and inescapably.[4]

At the present stage of the discussion we shall assume that the correct text of Matthew 19:9 reads as follows: λέγω δὲ ὑμῖν ὅτι ὃς ἂν ἀπολύσῃ τὴν γυναῖκα αὐτοῦ μὴ ἐπὶ πορνείᾳ καὶ γαμήσῃ ἄλλην, μοιχᾶται. The matter of textual variation will be discussed later. On the above reading of the text it may be well in passing to note some of its distinctive characteristics.

(a) This text does not reflect upon the character of the man's sin if he puts away his wife (for any other cause than that of adultery) but does not himself remarry. As found already, Matthew 5:32 deals very directly and decisively with that question and views the sin of the man from the standpoint of his reponsibility in the entail of consequence involved for the divorced woman. In Matthew 19:9, however, it is the sin of the man who contracts another marriage after illicit divorce which is the express subject of our Lord's judgment.

(b) The man who puts away his wife (except for fornication) and marries another is expressly condemned as an adulterer. This is an inference properly drawn from Matthew 5:32 but here it is directly stated.

(c) The rights of a woman in divorcing her husband for adultery and the sin of the woman who remarries after divorce

---

[4] It has been maintained that in Matthew 19:9, as also in Matthew 5:32, Jesus is not dealing with the dissolution of the marriage bond but only with the termination of a betrothal contract which had not yet been consummated in marriage. This view is untenable. In the preceding context of both passages (Matt. 5:31; 19:7, 8; cf. Mark 10:3–5) explicit reference is made to the provisions of Deuteronomy 24:1–4, where the wife in question cannot be simply a betrothed woman. Matthew 5:32 and 19:9 were spoken in direct reference to the question posed by Deuteronomy 24:1–4 and hence the relationship expressed by the word "wife" in Matthew 19:9 cannot be different from that supplied by verses 7 and 8. If we supposed such a difference between the wife of verses 7 and 8 and the wife of verse 9, then the subject of discourse would have been abruptly changed and the contrast between our Lord's provision and the Mosaic permission would be eliminated. The terms of the contrast intimated by the formula, "But I say to you" require us to regard the relationship expressed by the word "wife" as the same in both cases. There are other reasons for rejecting this facile interpretation of Matthew 19:9 but they need not be argued.

for any other reason are not reflected on in this passage. Only in Mark 10:12 is there any express allusion to divorce action on the part of the woman and there, as we shall see later, no reference is made to the intrinsic right of divorce but only to the adulterous character of remarriage.

The real crux of the question in Matthew 19:9 is, however, the force of the exceptive clause, "except for fornication" (μὴ ἐπὶ πορνείᾳ). In the actual terms of the text the question is: does this exceptive clause apply to the words γαμήσῃ ἄλλην and therefore to μοιχᾶται as well as to the verb ἀπολύσῃ? There can be no question but the exceptive clause provides an exception to the wrong of putting away. The kind of wrong from which it relieves the husband is not intimated as in Matthew 5:32 but, like the latter passage, it does enunciate a liberty granted to the innocent husband. It does not intimate, any more than Matthew 5:32, that the man is *obligated* to divorce his wife in the event of adultery on her part. It simply accords the right or liberty. The question then is: does this exception, by way of right or liberty, extend to the remarriage of the divorcing husband as well as to the putting away? Obviously, if the right extends to the remarriage the husband in such a case is not implicated in the sin of adultery in the event of his remarriage.

On this question the professing church is sharply divided. On the one hand, there are those who claim that while Matthew 19:9 (as also Matthew 5:32) gives to the innocent husband the right to put away the wife who has committed adultery, yet this does not give any warrant for the dissolution of the marriage bond and for the remarriage of the guiltless spouse. In other words, adultery gives the right of separation from bed and board (*a thoro et mensa*) but does not sever the bond of marriage nor does it give the right to dissolve that bond. Perhaps most notable in maintaining this position is the Roman Catholic Church. The position should not, however, be regarded as distinctively Romish. The distinguished Latin father, Augustine, can be enlisted in support of this interpretation.[5] Canon law of the Church of England, while allowing *separation* for adultery, does not permit of

[5] See *De Bono Conjugali, Lib.* I, *Capp.* VII, XV; *cf. In Joannis Evangelium, Tractatus* IX, 2.

remarriage for the parties so separated as long as they both live.[6]

If the text of Matthew 19:9, quoted above, is adopted as the genuine and authentic text, then there is considerable difficulty in holding to this position. The reason is apparent. It is the difficulty of restricting the exceptive clause to the putting away (ἀπολύσῃ) and not extending it also to the

[6] See Charles Gore: *The Question of Divorce* (London, 1911), pp. 1–11. Gore quotes from *Constitutions and Canons Ecclesiastical*, Canon 107, as follows:

"In all sentences for divorce, bond to be taken for not marrying during each other's life.

"In all sentences pronounced only for divorce and separation *a thoro et mensa*, there shall be a caution and restraint inserted in the act of the said sentence, that the parties so separated shall live chastely and continently; neither shall they, during each other's life, contract matrimony with any other person. And, for the better observation of this last clause, the said sentence of divorce shall not be pronounced until the party or parties requiring the same have given good and sufficient caution and security into the court, that they will not any way break or transgress the said restraint or prohibition" (pp. 5 f.). *Cf. Anglicanism*: Paul Elmer More and Frank Leslie Cross (Milwaukee, 1935), p. 661.

The Report of the Joint Committees of the Convocations of Canterbury and York, submitted in 1935, declared as follows on this subject: "The Church therefore will rightly teach its members that marriage is a calling for the whole of life, which asks for constant and unselfish effort. It will also say with much greater emphasis than in the past that believing Churchmen should reverently and advisedly marry believing Churchwomen, realising that grace to overcome their difficulties will be given to those who live their married life in the full fellowship of the Christian society. Further, in the case of two Church members who after every effort find it impossible to continue living together as man and wife, the Church will teach that they may separate, their separation being *a mensa et a toro*, but that it is against God's will for either to re-marry during the life-time of the other. Similarly, in the case of a Church member deserted or betrayed by an unworthy partner, the Church will counsel separation *a mensa et a toro*, and even in certain exceptional circumstances a legal dissolution of the marriage (which might be necessary, *e. g.*, for the protection of certain interests closely affecting the injured party or the children) but without re-marriage during the life-time of the former spouse" (*The Church and Marriage*, S. P. C. K., London, 1935, p. 18).

This position of the Church of England concerns simply Christian marriage and is not to be regarded as interfering with what is called the Pauline privilege (I Cor. 7:15). This question will be discussed later.

remarriage (γαμήσῃ ἄλλην).[7] This is, however, the construction that must be maintained if Matthew 19:9 is not interpreted as legitimating remarriage after divorce for adultery. The Romish Church is insistent that the exceptive clause modifies the first verb in the statement concerned but does not apply to the second. This exegesis is stated quite clearly by Aug. Lehmkuhl as follows:

> The complete exclusion of absolute divorce (*divortium perfectum*) in Christian marriage is expressed in the words quoted above Mark x; Luke xvi; I Cor. vii). The words in St. Matthew's Gospel (xix, 9), 'except it be for fornication', have, however, given rise to the question whether the putting away of the wife and the dissolution of the marriage bond were not allowed on account of adultery. The Catholic Church and Catholic theology have always maintained that by such an explanation St. Matthew would be made to contradict Sts. Mark, Luke, and Paul, and the converts instructed by these latter would have been brought into error in regard to the real doctrine of Christ. As this is inconsistent both with the infallibility of the Apostolic teaching and the inerrancy of Sacred Scripture, the clause in Matthew *must* be explained as the mere dismissal of the unfaithful wife without the dissolution of the marriage bond. Such a dismissal is not excluded by the parallel texts in Mark and Luke, while Paul (I Cor., vii, 11) clearly indicates the possibility of such a dismissal: 'And if she depart, that she remain unmarried, or be reconciled to her husband'. Grammatically, the clause in St. Matthew may modify one member of the sentence (that which refers to the putting away of the wife) without applying to the following member (the remarriage of the other), though we must admit that the construction is a little harsh. If it means, 'whoever shall put away his wife, except it be for fornication, and shall marry another, committeth adultery', then, in case of marital infidelity, the wife may be put away; but that, in this case, adultery is not committed by

---

[7] Such scholars as Charles Gore who deny the authenticity of the exceptive clause fully recognise that the exceptive clause applies to the remarriage as well as to the putting away. Gore says that the exceptive clause in Matthew 19:9 leaves "no doubt that divorce is used in such sense as covers permission to remarry" (*op. cit.*, p. 20; *cf.* p. 25). It is for this reason, in particular, that they seek to show the unhistoricity of the exceptive clause.

a new marriage cannot be concluded from these words. The following words, 'And he that shall marry her that is put away' — therefore also the woman who is dismissed for adultery — 'committeth adultery', say the contrary, since they suppose the permanence of the first marriage.[8]

[8] *The Catholic Encyclopedia*, Art. "Divorce", Vol. V, p. 56; *cf.* Arthur Devine: *The Law of Christian Marriage* (New York, 1908), p. 95. A most recent Roman Catholic work, *A Commentary on the New Testament* (1942), prepared by the Catholic Biblical Association, may here be quoted. "The teaching of Christ on divorce as recorded by the other Evangelists and understood by St. Paul (I Cor. 7, 10 f. 39; Rom. 7, 2) makes it perfectly clear that His prohibition of divorce with the right to remarry is absolute. Therefore the seeming exception mentioned in the First Gospel, *save on account of immorality* (5, 32), *except for immorality* (19, 9) cannot be understood in the sense that the innocent partner of an unfaithful spouse may divorce the guilty one and marry another person. The traditional interpretation of these words is undoubtedly correct: unfaithfulness justifies separation from bed and board, but the bond of marriage remains unbroken. St. Matthew records the words of Christ in their entirety. Our Lord had reason to mention this partial exception lest His absolute prohibition of divorce seem to imply that the injured party is obliged to continue to live with the unfaithful spouse. The other Evangelists, however, omit these words, probably intentionally, to forestall a false interpretation of them in the sense of permitting a divorce with the right to remarry" (pp. 52 f.).

It is not to be supposed that the Romish theory or practice in reference to the whole question of divorce is as simple or consistent as might appear. The Romish Church does sanction absolute divorce (*divortium a vinculo* distinguished, of course, from *divortium a thoro et mensa*) under certain conditions. In order to understand, however, the very elements of the Romish position it is necessary to appreciate the several distinctions between marriage, *legitimate*, *ratum*, and *consummatum*. In the words of Arthur Devine, "A marriage is called *legitimate* when contracted according to law by unbaptized persons. Such are the valid marriages of infidels. It is called *ratum* when validly contracted by those who are baptized, and is ratified by the Church. It is called *consummatum* when those validly married have used their conjugal rights" (*op. cit.*, pp. 44 f.). Rome teaches that a marriage that is only legitimate, even though consummated, may be dissolved in accordance with the Pauline privilege (I Cor. 7:15). There may not be any conspicuous inconsistency in this concession. But Rome also teaches that a marriage that is *ratum* but not *consummatum* may be dissolved in one of two ways: (1) by "profession of solemn vows in a religious order approved by the Church; (2) by the dispensation of the Sovereign Pontiff" (*ibid.* p. 89). It is here that the indefensible inconsistency and the presumption of Rome appear. There is no Scripture warrant for any such exceptions, and it is passing strange that Rome should be so

This construction of Matthew 19:9 is admitted to be "a little harsh" even by the foregoing apologist for the Romish interpretation. We shall see that this is very much of an understatement.

It must indeed be allowed that an exceptive clause is sometimes used in the Greek to intimate "an exception to something that is more general than that which has actually been mentioned".[9] We have examples of this use of εἰ μή in Matthew 12:4; Romans 14:14 and probably in Galatians 1:19. In such a case the exception stated here (μὴ ἐπὶ πορνείᾳ) would not be an exception to the principle that whosoever puts away his wife and marries another commits adultery but simply an exception to the principle that a man may not put away his wife. Consequently the real intent of the whole sentence would be, "But I say to you that whoever puts away his wife and marries another commits adultery — only, a man may *put away* his wife for the cause of fornication". Such a rendering does in itself make good sense and would solve a good many difficulties in harmonising the accounts given in the three synoptic Gospels. The question remains, however: is this construction defensible? There are preponderant reasons for rejecting it.

(1) If the exceptive clause is of the sort indicated above, namely, not an exception to that which is expressly stated but an exception to another closely related and more general consideration, then this is a most unusual, if not unparalleled,

jealous to maintain the absolute indissolubility of consummated marriage within the Roman Catholic Church and yet make such specious concessions in the interests of religious orders and by papal dispensation. All this stems from the insolent claim of Rome that the Romish "Church is the only authoritative and infallible teacher of faith and morals for all times and places" (*ibid*. pp. 94 f.).

With respect to marriage *ratum* and *consummatum*, Rome teaches that such can be dissolved only by the death of one of the parties.

For the official pronouncements of Rome see *Canons and Decrees of the Council of Trent*, Session XXIV, "Canons on the Sacrament of Matrimony", especially Canons 6 and 7.

[9] J. G. Machen: *Christianity Today*, October, 1931, p. 12. *Cf*. J. H. Thayer: *Greek-English Lexicon*, εἰ, III, 8, c, β; E. De Witt Burton: *A Critical and Exegetical Commentary on the Epistle to the Galatians* (New York, 1920), p. 60.

way of expressing it. In other instances where we have this
kind of exception the construction is quite different from that
in our text. In these other instances the statement of that to
which a more general exception is appended is given first in
its completeness and then the exception in its completeness
follows. But this is not the case here — the exception is inserted before the statement is completed. Analogy does not,
therefore, favour this rendering.

(2) While it is true grammatically that an exceptive clause
may modify one member of a sentence without modifying
another, yet it must be noted that, in this particular case, the
one member which the exceptive clause, on the Romish construction, is supposed to modify does not and cannot stand
alone in the syntax of the sentence concerned. Even if we
eliminate the clause καὶ γαμήσῃ ἄλλην from any modification by the exceptive clause we have not reached any solution
as far as the grammatical structure is concerned. In order to
complete the sense of what is introduced by the clause ὃς ἂν
ἀπολύσῃ τὴν γυναῖκα αὐτοῦ we must move on to the principal verb, namely, μοιχᾶται. But if we do this without
reference to the remarriage clause (καὶ γαμήσῃ ἄλλην) we
get nonsense and untruth, namely, "whoever puts away his
wife except for fornication commits adultery". In other
words, it must be observed that in this sentence as it stands
no thought is complete without the principal verb, μοιχᾶται.
It is this thought of committing adultery by remarriage that
is the ruling thought in this passage, and it is quite indefensible
to suppress it. The very exceptive clause, therefore, must
have direct bearing upon the action denoted by the verb that
governs. But in order to have direct bearing upon the governing verb (μοιχᾶται) it must also have direct bearing upon
that which must occur before the action denoted by the
principal verb can take effect, namely, the marrying of another. This direct bearing which the exceptive clause must
have on the remarriage and on the committing of adultery is
simply another way of saying that, as far as the syntax of the
sentence is concerned, the exceptive clause must apply to
the committing of adultery in the event of remarriage as well
as to the wrong of putting away.

A comparison with Matthew 5:32 will help to clarify this

point. There it is said, "Everyone who puts away his wife except for the cause of fornication makes her to commit adultery". In this case the exceptive clause has full meaning and relevance apart altogether from remarriage on the part of the divorcing husband. This is so because the sin contemplated on the part of the divorcing husband is not the committing of adultery on his part but the making of his wife to be an adulteress. But in Matthew 19:9 the case is entirely different. The burden thought here in 19:9 is the committing of adultery on the part of the divorcing husband himself. But this sin on his part presupposes his remarriage. Consequently, in the syntax of the sentence as it actually is, the meaning and relevance of the exceptive clause cannot be maintained apart from its application to the remarriage as well as to the putting away.

(3) What is contemplated in this sentence is not merely putting away, as in Matthew 5:31, 32, but putting away and remarriage on the part of the husband. In this respect it is to be carefully distinguished from the *logion* of Matt. 5:32 and must be placed in the same category as Mark 10:11 and Luke 16:18. The subject dealt. with, therefore, is putting away and remarriage in coordination, and this coordination must not be disturbed in any way. It is this coordination that leads up to and prepares the ground for the principal verb, namely, the committing of adultery on the part of the divorcing husband. It would be unwarranted, therefore, to relate the exceptive clause to anything else than the coordination. Furthermore, the exceptive clause is in the natural position with reference to the coordination and with reference to the resulting sin to which it provides an exception. Where else could the exceptive clause be placed if it applies to all three elements of the situation expressed? And if it is in the natural position as applying to the coordination the natural construction is that it contemplates an exception to the statement of the sentence in its entirety.

(4) The divorce permitted or tolerated under the Mosaic economy had the effect of dissolving the marriage bond. This Mosaic permission regarding divorce is referred to in the context of this passage as well as in Matthew 5:31 and in the parallel passage in Mark 10:2–12. In each of these cases

the same verb (ἀπολύω) is used with reference to this Mosaic provison.[10] Now since this was the effect of the divorce alluded to in this passage and since there is not the slightest indication that the actual putting away for adultery, legitimated in Matthew 19:9; 5:32, was to have an entirely different effect, we are surely justified in concluding that the putting away sanctioned by our Lord was intended to have the same effect in the matter of dissolving the marriage tie. It should be appreciated that the law as enunciated here by Jesus does not in any way suggest any alteration in the nature and effect of divorce. The change intimated by Jesus was rather the abolition of every other reason permitted in the Mosaic provisions and the distinct specification that adultery was now the only ground upon which a man could legitimately put away his wife. What is abrogated then is not divorce with its attendant dissolution of the marriage bond but rather all ground for divorce except adultery.

If divorce involves dissolution of the marriage bond, then we should not expect that remarriage would be regarded as adultery.

(5) It is surely reasonable to assume that if the man may legitimately put away his wife for adultery the marriage bond is judged to be dissolved. On any other supposition the woman who has committed adultery and who has been put away is still in reality the man's wife and is one flesh with him. If so it would appear very anomalous that the man should have the right to put away one who is permanently, while life lasts, wife and is one flesh with him. To take action that relieves of the obligations of matrimony while the marital tie is inviolate hardly seems compatible with marital ethics as taught in the Scripture itself. It is true that Paul distinctly contemplates the possibility of separation

---

[10] In the Old Testament passages in which divorce is mentioned or referred to (Lev. 21:7, 14; 22:13; Numb. 30:10; Deut. 22:19, 29; 24:1–4; Isa. 50:1; Jer. 3:1; Ezek. 44:22) the Septuagint does not use the verb ἀπολύω. It uses the verbs ἐκβάλλω and ἐξαποστέλλω. This should not, however, be regarded as implying any substantial difference. The verb ἀπολύω is used in the New Testament accounts with reference to the Old Testament provision of Deuteronomy 24:1–4, even though in the latter passage it is the verb ἐξαποστέλλω that is used in every case.

without dissolution and propounds what the law is in such a contingency (I Cor. 7:10, 11). But to provide for and sanction permanent separation while the marriage tie remains inviolate is something that is alien to the whole tenor of Scripture teaching in regard to the obligations that inhere in and are inseparable from the marital bond.

(6) The position that adultery warrants putting away but not dissolution of the marriage bond would appear to conflict with another principle of Scripture that applies to the aggravated case of harlotry or prostitution. If adultery does not give ground for dissolution of the marriage bond, then a man may not secure dissolution even when his wife has abandoned herself to prostitution. This seems quite contrary to the principle of purity expressed by the apostle (I Cor. 6:15–17). It would appear, therefore, that dissolution of the marriage bond must be the proper means and, in some cases, the mandatory means of securing release from a bond that binds so uniquely to one who is thus defiled.

On these various grounds we may conclude that it is not feasible to construe the exceptive clause of Matthew 19:9 as applying merely to the putting away and not to the remarriage on the part of the divorcing husband. The considerations preponderate rather in favour of the conclusion that when a man puts away his wife for the cause of fornication this putting away has the effect of dissolving the bond of marriage with the result that he is free to remarry without thereby incurring the guilt of adultery. In simple terms it means that divorce in such a case dissolves the marriage and that the parties are no longer man and wife.

Mark 10:2–12; Luke 16:18

The first question that arises in connection with Mark 10:2–12 is the apparent discrepancy between Matthew 19:7, 8, on the one hand, and Mark 10:3–5, on the other. In Matthew 19:7 we are told that the Pharisees asked the question, "Why then did Moses command to give a bill of divorce and to put away?" Jesus in reply said, "Moses for your hardness of heart suffered you to put away your wives". The difference between the form of the Pharisees' question and our Lord's reply has been discussed already and the significance of the

word Jesus used, namely, *suffered* duly noted. But in Mark
10:3–5 the terms appear to be reversed. Jesus asks, "What
did Moses *command* you?" and the Pharisees replied, "Moses
suffered to write a bill of divorce and to put away". Again
Jesus replied, "For your hardness of heart he wrote you this
commandment" (τὴν ἐντολὴν ταύτην). So in Matthew's
account the Pharisees use the word indicative of command
(ἐνετείλατο) and Jesus uses the word expressive of permission (ἐπέτρεψεν). In the account in Mark Jesus uses words
indicative of command (ἐνετείλατο and ἐντολή) whereas
the Pharisees use the word expressive of permission (ἐπέτρεψεν). Furthermore, the account in Mark might appear to
upset the line of interpretation offered earlier with respect
to the exact significance of the Mosaic provision in Deuteronomy 24:1–4. The discrepancy is, however, not real and
may rather readily be resolved. The following considerations
may be adduced.

(1) It is entirely possible that the word "command" in
Jesus' question of Mark 10:3 may not have been intended to
refer merely to Deuteronomy 24:1–4. By the question, "What
did Moses command you?" he may have had in mind the
whole of the Mosaic revelation and may well be regarded as
pointing to Genesis 2:24 as well as Deuteronomy 24:1–4.
Such an interpretation would carry no suggestion that Moses
commanded the Israelites to put away their wives under
certain contingencies. The question could well be regarded
as equivalent to, "What were the Mosaic provisions on this
matter?"

(2) Even if it be granted that the allusion in Jesus' question of Mark 10:3 is to Deuteronomy 24:1–4, it does not at
all follow that Jesus construes the Deuteronomic provision
as requiring men to put away their wives. The question,
"What did Moses command you?" may simply mean, "What
was the Mosaic legislation on this question?" and it would
be an entirely unwarranted importation into the question to
suppose that this implied that Deuteronomy 24:1 required
men to put away their wives in the event of the unclean thing
specified. Neither does the question carry even the implication that Moses authorised or sanctioned the divorce.

The same holds true with respect to the words, "this commandment" (τὴν ἐντολὴν ταύτην) in Mark 10:5. The antecedent of this expression is the statement of the Pharisees in the preceding verse, "Moses permitted to write a bill of divorce and to put away". It should be noted that Jesus does not say anything to dispute the Pharisees' statement of the case. He rather endorses their statement by his answer. In any case, it would be importing far too much into his use of the word, "precept" (ἐντολή) to understand it as implying, "Moses did not simply permit to write a bill of divorce and to put away: he also required you to write a bill of divorce and to put away". The reasonable view is that Jesus is simply using the word, "precept" as a designation of the legislative, regulatory enactment of Deuteronomy 24:1–4 without in the least intimating that the divorce itself was mandatory.

(3) We must bear in mind that there were certain positive requirements in the Mosaic provision of Deuteronomy 24:1–4. Though it did not imply that divorce was mandatory, yet it did imply that if a divorce were given then certain strict requirements had to be followed. This consideration may well be the reason why Jesus refers to the Deuteronomic provision in verse 5 in terms of precept and in verse 3, quite possibly, in terms of command. The provision as a whole is a most definite prescription, even though every element or condition mentioned should not be construed as prescription.

It may be impossible to arrange all the details of the two accounts into exact chronological sequence. We may not have sufficient information by which to reconstruct the whole episode. But it should be perceived that there is no contradiction between the two accounts as found in Matthew 19:7, 8, and Mark 10:3–5. The latter passage, therefore, does not provide any warrant for departing from the interpretation of Deuteronomy 24:1–4 given earlier or for any revision of our estimate of the corroboration given to this interpretation by Matthew 19:7, 8.

The second and far more important question that emerges in connection with Mark 10:2–12 is the omission of the exceptive clause in Mark 10:11. The same is true of Luke 16:18. In both Mark and Luke there is no exception to the rule, "Whoever puts away his wife and marries another commits adultery", whereas in Matthew 19:9 there is the one exception, namely, for the cause of fornication.

It is not within the scope of these studies to enter into the debate concerning source criticism. There are critics who are willing to grant on the basis of the manuscript evidence that the exceptive clause belongs to the text of Matthew's Gospel and who, at the same time, have no scruple in denying its authenticity as a genuine part of our Lord's *logion* on this question. For example, G. H. Box in his booklet *Divorce in the New Testament*, written jointly with Charles Gore in answer to R. H. Charles,[11] says, "In the Markan account, and also in Luke xvi. 18, the prohibition of divorce is absolute. In Matthew (xix. 9, *cf.* v. 32) a limiting clause is introduced, *except for fornication* or *unchastity.* This clearly is a case of editorial addition or modification. It formed no part of our Lord's teaching in its original form, which is preserved correctly in Mark and Luke. Dr. Charles, in fact, admits that it is a gloss, introduced into the text by the compiler of the first Gospel. But he contends that it is a correct gloss, intended to guard the passage from misinterpretation. The argument by which he justifies this contention we shall proceed to examine."[12] The insertion of the exceptive clause, Box says

[11] R. H. Charles: *The Teaching of the New Testament on Divorce* (London, 1921). Dr. Charles takes the position that the exceptive clause in Matthew 19:9 is an editorial addition by Matthew and is not an actual word of the Lord himself. Nevertheless he thinks that this addition by Matthew was perfectly justifiable in order properly to convey our Lord's teaching on the subject. The *words* of our Lord are properly reported in Mark and have no exceptive clause. When the words were spoken, Charles avers, the Old Testament law requiring death for adultery was still in force and consequently the exception in the case of adultery would have been perfectly understood. However, this law relating to the infliction of death was abrogated a few years later. Accordingly Matthew, writing after the abrogation of this law and recognising that the actual words of our Lord would or might have been gravely misunderstood, "edited the narrative afresh and inserted the clause, 'saving for the cause of unchastity' " in order truly to convey our Lord's thought and teaching. Matthew then, according to Charles, departs from the actual *logion* of Christ and adds the exceptive clause. But in so doing he saved the actual meaning of our Lord from grave misconception (see pp. 22 ff.). It is this position of Charles that G. H. Box and Charles Gore vigorously controvert. For a more recent and rather thorough discussion of this question see Felix L. Cirlot: *Christ and Divorce* (Lexington, Ky., 1945).

[12] London, 1921, p. 18.

further, "is no doubt due to the editor of the Gospel in its final shape, and was intended to exclude from Christ's words the special case of adultery. Divorce for proved adultery, and remarriage for the innocent husband, is thus allowed in the text of these passages, though not, as we hold with the authority of Christ. The words were inserted by the editor, and doubtless reflect the current practice of the Palestinian Church when he wrote."[13] On such a hypothesis the apparent contradiction is removed from our Lord's teaching and remains simply in diverse accounts of what Christ said.

We are not able to adopt this critical solution. We are compelled to take the position that if the exceptive clause belongs to the genuine text of Matthew's Gospel, then it truly represents our Lord's teaching. It would be incompatible with the inspiration of Scripture to reject Matthew in favour of Mark and Luke, as it would also be to reject Mark and Luke in favour of Matthew. If the genuine texts of the three Gospels retain the apparent contradiction, then some other method than that of the denial of the authenticity of one or the other must be adopted.

There is, however, a textual variant in Matthew 19:9 which, if adopted as the genuine text, would remove the discrepancy.

[13] *Ibid.* p. 39. Charles Gore, ten years earlier, in *The Question of Divorce* took the same position. He says, "What appears to be the case is that the First Gospel 'according to Matthew' was compiled in some Jewish-Christian community, probably in Palestine, at a date which cannot be much later at any rate than the destruction of Jerusalem, and was based upon the Gospel of St. Mark and the (originally Aramaic) recollections of St. Matthew as well as upon other materials. It would appear that in this Jewish community, where it originated, the old Jewish feeling had been allowed to assert itself so far as to modify in respect of marriage the original strictness of our Lord's command. No doubt the exceptive clause as it appears in the first Gospel was believed to express the real intention of Christ — 'what He must have meant.' But it cannot be admitted that this was really the case. So serious an exception must have been expressed. The law with the exception is really a different law from the law without exception.

"It must be added that the critical conclusion that the exceptive clause in the first Gospel is an interpolation, which really alters the sense of our Lord's original utterance about marriage, and that His real teaching is that given in St. Mark's and St. Luke's Gospels, represents an impressive consensus of scholars from Germany, France, America, and our own country . . ." (pp. 22 f.).

This variant, instead of reading μὴ ἐπὶ πορνεία καὶ γαμήσῃ ἄλλην, μοιχᾶται, reads as follows: παρεκτὸς λόγου πορνείας, ποιεῖ αὐτὴν μοιχευθῆναι. It is apparent that this reading removes the discrepancy between Matthew 19:9 and Mark 10:11; Luke 16:18 for the simple reason that all reference to remarriage would be removed from Matthew 19:9 and this text would be identical in meaning with Matthew 5:32. In such a case the accounts in Matthew would simply affirm that there is one exception to the rule that whoever puts away his wife causes her to commit adultery, namely, antecedent adultery on the part of the wife herself. But nothing whatsoever would be said regarding the remarriage of the man who puts away his wife for adultery. On the other hand, the accounts in Mark and Luke would deal directly with the question of the remarriage of the man who puts away his wife and would affirm that whoever puts away his wife, whether for adultery or for any other cause, and marries another, commits adultery. The whole case could then be summed up in a few words: a man may put away his wife for adultery, though for that reason alone, but in no case may a man put away his wife and marry another. Matthew states the former on two occasions, Mark and Luke state the latter. No discrepancy remains and so further harmonisation is unnecessary.

The question remains however: which of these readings is to be adopted as the genuine text? The problem is not by any means simple. The very fact that the two important fourth century uncials, Codex Sinaiticus (א) and Codex Vaticanus (B), are on opposite sides indicates the difficulty.

It is not without significance that critical editors of the Greek text of the New Testament such as Tischendorf, Westcott and Hort, von Soden, Nestle, and Souter have preferred the reading, μὴ ἐπὶ πορνείᾳ καὶ γαμήσῃ ἄλλην, μοιχᾶται and have this variant in the actual text of their editions of the New Testament. And the English Revised (1881), the American Revised (1901) and the American Revised Standard (1946), as well as the Authorised (1611), versions in English have followed this reading.

It is not without good reason that these editors of the Greek text and the English translations referred to have cast

their vote in this way. While any detailed analysis of the
evidence bearing upon this textual question hardly falls
within the scope of these studies and would be beyond the
capacity of the present writer, yet a brief summation of
reasons leading to the conclusion that the above reading is
the preferred text is not only in order but also necessary. The
following observations may be adduced:

(i) As regards the external evidence there is a distinctly
impressive array of uncial and cursive manuscripts and also
of versions in support of the reading just quoted as the preferred text. While the mere number of manuscripts and
versions does not of itself settle a textual question, yet the
variety as well as the mass in this particular case constrains
the conclusion that very cogent reasons would have to be
presented if it were to be rejected as the proper reading.
Such reasons do not appear to reside in the opposing evidence.

(ii) The alternative reading supported by Codex Vaticanus
(B), namely, παρεκτὸς λόγου πορνείας ποιεῖ αὐτὴν μοιχευθῆναι must not be considered in its entirety but rather
in its two distinct component clauses, when the external evidence in its favour is being evaluated. When this is done it
will be found that the evidence in support of the second clause,
ποιεῖ αὐτὴν μοιχευθῆναι is not as strong as that in support
of the first, παρεκτὸς λόγου πορνείας. For example, while
Codex Vaticanus is supported by Codex Bezae in the reading
παρεκτὸς λόγου πορνείας it is not supported by Codex
Bezae in the reading ποιεῖ αὐτὴν μοιχευθῆναι. At this point
Codex Bezae rather supports Codex Sinaiticus and reads καὶ
γαμήσῃ ἄλλην. And the same holds true of a goodly number
of Latin manuscripts.

It should be noted that, as far as the sense of the passage is
concerned, it is not the reading παρεκτὸς λόγου πορνείας
that is crucial; as far as meaning is concerned this has the
same effect as μὴ ἐπὶ πορνείᾳ. It is the second clause, ποιεῖ
αὐτὴν μοιχευθῆναι that makes the crucial difference. And
it is surely significant that, although B enlists a good deal of
collateral support in the clause that makes no difference to
the sense, it decidedly loses support in the clause that introduces crucial divergence in the meaning of the passage. In
other words, the reading of B weakens the farther it goes in

assimilation to Matthew 5:32 and the farther it proceeds in changing the entire force of the passage.

(iii) From the viewpoint of transcriptional probability the reading μὴ ἐπὶ πορνείᾳ καὶ γαμήσῃ ἄλλην, μοιχᾶται is decidedly the more difficult. It is so because it appears to contradict Mark 10:11; Luke 16:18. Hence, if this reading represents the genuine text of Matthew 19:9 it is easy to understand why the other reading should have crept in — removal of the discrepancy between Matthew 19:9 and Mark 10:11; Luke 16:18, and assimilation to Matthew 5:32. On the other hand, if the genuine text of Matthew 19:9 should read as Matthew 5:32 it is very difficult to see why the other reading would have crept in. It should be appreciated that if the text of Matthew 19:9 reads as we have been contending, then it is wholly unique in the New Testament. This uniqueness argues for its genuineness rather than for the opposite.

(iv) Evidence of assimilation to Matthew 5:32 in the reading supported by B appears not only in the clauses we have been considering but also in the latter part of Matthew 19:9, καὶ ὁ ἀπολελυμένην γαμήσας μοιχᾶται.[14] There appears, therefore, to be a sustained pattern of assimilation to Matthew 5:32 in this reading. This feature, when related to all the factors involved, is a count against its genuineness rather than in its favour.

For such reasons as these we conclude, therefore, that the balance of the considerations supports the judgment that the reading μὴ ἐπὶ πορνείᾳ καὶ γαμήσῃ ἄλλην, μοιχᾶται is the genuine text of Matthew 19:9 and that the apparent discrepancy between Mark 10:11; Luke 16:18 and Matthew 19:9 cannot feasibly be resolved by the adoption of the variant reading that assimilates Matthew 19:9 to 5:32. Hence

---

[14] The question of the genuineness of this latter part of Matthew 19:9 will not be discussed now. There is, of course, no question regarding the genuineness of the practically equivalent statements in Matthew 5:32; Luke 16:18. Suffice it to say that if we follow the judgment of several critical editors of the Greek text that this part of Matthew 19:9 is not genuine, then the argument given above is greatly strengthened. In the opinion of the present writer, the argument against the reading of B in Matthew 19:9, namely, assimilation to 5:32, may be strengthened by consideration of the latter part of Matthew 19:9 even if this latter part is genuine.

we are compelled to face anew the question of harmonisation. Matthew 19:9 enunciates one exception to the rule that if a man puts away his wife and marries another he commits adultery; Mark and Luke do not enunciate any such exception. Is there a real contradiction here between the Synoptists? The resolution of this question appears to lie along the following lines.

(1) We must bear in mind that the burden of the emphasis in this discourse of our Lord, in the form in which it appears both in Matthew 19:3–9 and in Mark 10:2–12, is upon the abrogation of the Mosaic permission of Deuteronomy 24:1–4. Since there was no provision for divorce for adultery in the law of Moses the passages in Matthew and Mark involve a complete annulment of the permission granted for other reasons and presupposed in this Deuteronomic passage. Now, in both Mark and Luke the form of statement used focuses attention upon that fact. As far as the Mosaic provisions regarding divorce are concerned the law enunciated by Jesus, in the form of Matthew 19:9 as well as in the form of Mark 10:11; Luke 16:18, is quite absolute. In other words, there is no exception to the abrogation of the permission implied in Deuteronomy 24:1–4. Not even Matthew 19:9 allows for that kind of exception. The absolute form of statement in Mark 10:11; Luke 16:18 stresses most pointedly the abrogation of the Mosaic provision in this particular and Matthew 19:9 does not in any way modify or retract such abrogation.

(2) It should be noted that there is no mention either in Mark or in Luke of the right of a man to put away his wife for adultery. This is a remarkable omission, particularly in Mark, in view of the greater detail with which he reports our Lord's teaching at this point. There can be no question, however, about the propriety of such dismissal. It is clearly established by Matthew 5:32 and also by Matthew 19:9 on whatever reading we regard as genuine. We have no reason to suppose that Mark and Luke intended to deny such a right and there is no suggestion of its illegitimacy. Yet neither Mark nor Luke makes any allusion to this liberty granted by Matthew 5:32; 19:9. Since, then, the silence of Mark and Luke respecting this right does not in any way prejudice the right itself, to say the least may we not properly suspect that

the omission on their part of any reference to the right of remarriage, in the case of the man who divorces his wife for adultery, was not intended to prejudice or deny that right?

(3) Furthermore, since Mark and Luke do not refer to *divorce for adultery* they could not in the nature of the case refer to the *right of remarriage* in the event of such divorce. It is obvious that the latter, if legitimate, rests upon the former. And since their silence regarding the former does not exclude its legitimacy nor does it imply that they were unaware of its legitimacy, why should we insist that their silence regarding the latter *necessarily* excludes its legitimacy or even their knowledge of its legitimacy, particularly since their silence regarding the former *necessarily* precluded any reference to the latter.

We may reasonably conclude, therefore, that Mark and Luke are not envisaging the situation created in the event of adultery and are not reflecting on the rights of the innocent spouse in such a case. They are concentrating rather upon the abrogation of certain Mosaic provisions anent divorce and upon prevalent customs in both Jewish and Gentile circles. They report our Lord's teaching as it was directed to these specific evils. Matthew does likewise. But the latter conveys to us additional information regarding our Lord's teaching on this question, namely, his teaching bearing upon the contingency of adultery. Matthew informs us of two things: (a) a man may put away his wife for adultery; (b) he may marry another when such divorce is consummated.

The third notable difference that appears in Mark 10:2–12, when compared with the parallel passage in Matthew, is Mark 10:12. Up to this point in our discussion the right of divorce in the case of adultery has been predicated exclusively of the man as distinguished from the woman. As stated already, it is only in Matthew that the right of divorce for adultery is intimated, but in both instances (5:32; 19:9) there is no reference to the rights of the woman in the event of adultery on the part of her husband. Quite naturally we are led to inquire if good and necessary inference based on other principles of Scripture does not require the extension of the right of divorce to the woman. It is for this reason that Mark 10:12 is so instructive and important, for, at least so far as the Gospels are concerned, this is the only passage in which there is allusion to divorce on the part of the woman. "And if she, having put away her husband, marry another, she commits adultery."

It must indeed be recognised that Mark does not here speak of the right of the woman to put away her husband in the event of adultery on his part. As noted already, Mark does not anywhere reflect on the right of divorce for adultery. And it would be quite unjustifiable to infer that there is here any intent to allude to such a right on the part of the woman. The ostensible import of Mark 10:12 is that the same law applies to the woman as applies to the man if she takes the initiative in a divorce suit. The significant feature, however, of Mark 10:12 is that it contemplates the possibility of divorce on the part of the woman and therefore presupposes such an eventuality. This means that the social order as envisaged by this passage in Mark is one in which divorce proceedings may be instituted by the woman as well as by the man.[15]

---

[15] It has been argued that Mark 10:12 is not an authentic word of our Lord but that Mark adapted or amplified our Lord's teaching to the conditions prevailing in the Graeco-Roman world. Heinrich Meyer, for example, says: "The narrative of Mark is certainly not original (in opposition to Schenkel), but puts into the mouth of Jesus what was the custom among the *Greeks* and *Romans*, namely, that the wife also might be the divorcing party, and very often actually was so, which was not competent to the *Jewish* wife (Deut. xxiv. 1; Josephus, *Antt.* xv. 7.10), for the instances of *Michal* (I Sam. xxv. 41), of *Herodias* (Matt. xiv. 4 f.), and of *Salome* (Josephus, *Antt.* xv. 7.10) are abnormal in respect to their rank; and the cases in which, according to the Rabbins, the wife might require that the husband should give her a writing of divorcement, do not belong to the question here, where the wife herself is the party who puts away. The proposition in the passage before us is derived from an *Hellenic* amplification of the tradition, which, however, in Matthew is again excluded" (*ad loc.*). *Cf.* P. W. Schmiedel in *Encyclopaedia Biblica*, (New York, 1903), Vol. II, col. 1851; R. H. Charles: *The Teaching of the New Testament on Divorce*, pp. 27–29. On the other hand it is just as strenuously argued that a reference to divorce on the part of the wife would be "singularly appropriate" at this time. F. C. Burkitt, for example, says: "This condemnation of the woman is not found in Matthew and Luke, and it is pretty generally assumed to be a secondary addition, 'based on Roman Law,' says Dr. Schmiedel in *Encyclopaedia Biblica*, col. 1851. I venture to think such a view mistaken, and that so far from being a secondary addition it is one of the really primitive features of the Gospel of Mark, a feature which was dropped out or altered when its historical meaning had been forgotten." Burkitt then proceeds to instance the case of Herodias and concludes:

There can be no doubt then that our Lord here enunciates
a law or principle which applies to a situation in which divorce
by the woman as well as by the man is recognised as belonging to the actual *status quo*.

This text does not of itself prove that the right of the man
to divorce his wife for adultery, established by Matthew 5:32;
19:9, belongs also in like manner to the woman. But it does
point in the direction of a distinct provision in the Christian
economy to the effect that the woman is accorded an equal
right with the man in the event of marital unfaithfulness on
the part of her spouse. In the Old Testament there is no provision for divorce by the woman. There does not appear to
be any such provision in Jewish custom at the time of our
Lord.[16] But in this saying (Mark 10:12) there is an indication that our Lord in the exercise of the authority that be-
longed to him not only provided that a man may divorce his
wife for the cause of fornication but that the wife also may
divorce her husband for the same offence.[17]

"Our Lord's previous words show that he did not regard an immoral act
as being any the less immoral for being carried out according to law: in
either case I venture to think the saying as reported in Mark clearly implies
a reference to Herodias, a reference which is singularly appropriate in the
time and place" (*The Gospel History and its Transmission*, Edinburgh, 1906,
pp. 100 f.).

Suffice it to say here that it would be wholly indefensible to suppose
that our Lord confined himself, particularly in his more private instructions to his disciples as in this instance, to what would have strict and
exclusive appurtenance to Jewish custom. Furthermore, as H. B. Swete
points out, "the practice of the Pagan and Hellenised circles . . . must have
been already familiar to the Twelve" and with it "they would shortly be
called to deal" (*The Gospel According to St. Mark*, London, 1898, p. 206).
There is, therefore, no good reason for disputing the practical relevance,
far less the authenticity, of this saying.

[16] See Josephus: *Antiq. Jud.*, XV, vii, 10. Referring to Salome who sent
Costobarus her husband a bill of divorce and dissolved the marriage, he
says, "This was not according to the laws of the Jews. For with us it is
lawful for a husband to do this, but for a wife who has separated herself
it is not lawful for her to be married to another unless her former husband
put her away."

[17] The bearing of I Cor. 7:10–16 upon the question of the rights of the
woman in the Christian economy will be discussed later. Interesting reflec-
tions on this question from the early church will be found in *The Shepherd
of Hermas*, Mand. 4, I and Justin Martyr's *Second Apology*, Chap. II.

III

The Teaching of Paul

I Corinthians 7:10–15

In the preceding chapter the position was taken and argued that the exceptive clause of Matthew 19:9 is both genuine and authentic and that, therefore, the innocent husband is accorded the right not only to put away the wife who has committed adultery but also to marry another after the divorce from his former wife has been consummated. Those who controvert this position appeal not only to Mark 10:11; Luke 16:18, where no exceptive clause occurs, but also to I Corinthians 7:10, 11: "But to the married I give charge, not I but the Lord, that the wife depart not from her husband — but if she does depart, let her remain unmarried or be reconciled to her husband — and that the husband leave not his wife". The reason for such appeal to this Pauline deliverance is obvious; here it is distinctly provided that if, as a matter of fact, husband and wife have been separated from each other then they must remain unmarried or be reconciled. A case of separation without the right to remarry is clearly envisaged. Indeed, this passage expressly forbids remarriage on the part of either spouse. Hence it is concluded that while adultery gives to the innocent spouse the right to put away (*a thoro et mensa*), yet to neither spouse is accorded the right of remarriage.[1]

The appeal to this text in the interest of supporting such a position is singularly inconsistent. It is quite true that Paul here contemplates a case of separation and distinctly declares

[1] *Cf. A Commentary on the New Testament* (The Catholic Biblical Association, 1942), pp. 52 f.; Arthur Devine: *The Law of Christian Marriage* (New York, 1908), p. 93; Aug. Lehmkuhl in the article "Divorce" in *The Catholic Encyclopedia*, Vol. V, p. 56.

that the parties are to remain unmarried. But the relevance of this rule to the case of divorce for adultery is by no means apparent. The Romish exegetes, for example, who adduce this text in support of their position should have recognised that if this text has relevance to the case of divorce for adultery, then it proves far too much. For Paul here not only says that the spouses, in the event of actual separation, must remain unmarried but also that they should never have been separated. He declares unequivocally, "But to the married I give charge, not I but the Lord, that the wife depart not from her husband . . . and that the husband leave not his wife". If the rule of I Corinthians 7:10, 11 applies to the case of divorce for adultery, then it requires not only that the spouses, if separated, remain unmarried but also that separation should not by any means take effect. In other words, it would not simply be remarriage that would be prohibited but also the mildest kind of divorce. It must be observed that the primary emphasis of this text is not the parenthetical clauses — "but if she does depart, let her remain unmarried or be reconciled to her husband" — but the prohibition of separation, a prohibition invested with the authority of none other than the Lord himself. Yet, inconsistently enough, this text is adduced in support of the position that an innocent spouse may properly dismiss the adulterous spouse but may not remarry as long as the dismissed spouse lives. This is plainly an example of appeal to one part of a text in neglect of the clear import of the other part, and, in this instance, of appeal to the part that is distinctly subordinate and contingent in neglect of the part that is unconditional and primary. The upshot simply is that if this text bears upon the question of divorce for adultery such divorce is expressly forbidden, and forbidden, be it noted, not only in the sense of dissolution of the marriage bond but also in the sense of separation from bed and board.

Such a conclusion, however, cannot be admitted. For Matthew 5:32; 19:9 clearly establish the right of divorce for adultery, and even those who deny the legitimacy of dissolving the bond of marriage in such a case nevertheless fully admit the right of divorce from bed and board. What then is to be our conclusion regarding I Corinthians 7:10, 11? Interpreters

who do not accept the authenticity of the exceptive clause in
Matthew 5:32; 19:9 have no difficulty. They say that Paul
followed the tradition represented by Mark 10:11; Luke 16:18.
This tradition they claim allows for no exception and repro-
duces the authentic teaching of our Lord. Paul, consequently,
allows for no exception. Reasons have already been presented
for the rejection of this solution. So we shall have to look in
another direction for the resolution of this question.

Unless we are to suppress the clear teaching of I Corinthians
7:10, 11 or bring its teaching into conflict with the express
provisions of Matthew 5:32; 19:9, the only alternative is to
conclude that Paul is not here dealing with the case of adultery. And it is surely not difficult to find the reason or reasons
why Paul is not bringing within the scope of his teaching the
provisions that obtain in the event of adultery on the part of
a spouse. In the preceding verses the great burden of Paul's
exhortations is the means God has provided for the prevention
of fornication. "But on account of the fornications let each
man have his own wife, and let each woman have her own
husband" (vs. 2). "Do not defraud one another, except it be
by consent for a season in order that ye may give yourselves
to prayer and be together again, lest Satan tempt you on
account of your incontinence" (vs. 5). He is stressing the
ordinance of marriage and the conjugal debt that is owing
within the married relationship as the divine provisions for
the prevention of sexual uncleanness. Furthermore, he is
writing to the Corinthians as believers who are cognisant of,
and will be expected to be responsive to, the demands of the
Christian ethic. He is pleading for the claims of honour,
purity and piety in that relationship which had been so grossly
desecrated in their pagan antecedents and environment.
When all of this is duly assessed we can readily see how
incongruous it might be for the apostle in such a context to
introduce the question of the provisions that hold when the
marital relation is desecrated by sexual infidelity. Reflection
upon such a question would be outside the universe of his
discourse at this time, and, consequently, we need not be in
the least perplexed if the principles and rules enunciated in
this context do not bring within their purview the contingency
of adultery and the exceptive provisions that apply in that

event. We may conclude, therefore, that the omission of any
allusion to these exceptive provisions does not in any way
exclude such provisions and that the silence of the apostle
regarding the contingency of adultery does not presuppose
ignorance on his part respecting the provisions of Matthew
5:32; 19:9. With this assumption in mind, that the case of
adultery is outside the universe of discourse in this passage,
we may proceed to observe what the apostle enjoins.[2]

The strength of the injunction, "I give charge" ($\pi\alpha\rho$-
$\alpha\gamma\gamma\epsilon\lambda\lambda\omega$) is peculiarly evident. The apostle is enunciating
his apostolic authority; nothing less will measure up to the
weight of the word he uses. The clause immediately appended,
"Not I but the Lord" does not reduce the strength of his
own command; Paul is not retracting his assertion of authority
but rather reminding his readers that the charge he is giving
was already given by the Lord himself in the days of his
flesh. This appeal to the Lord is for the purpose of reinforce-
ment and is a direct allusion to the teaching of our Lord
recorded in Matthew 5:31, 32; 19:3–12; Mark 10:2–12; Luke
16:18 and transmitted, no doubt, at the time Paul wrote,
through authentic tradition.

The terms of the Pauline prohibition are quite absolute
and are in effect, "Let not the wife separate herself from her
husband, and let not the husband leave his wife".[3] The

---

[2] It must be understood, of course, that the main burden of our Lord's
teaching in Matthew 5:32; 19:9 is not outside the universe of discourse
of I Corinthians 7:10, 11. As was pointed out in an earlier chapter, it is not
the exception that bears the weight of the emphasis in Matthew 5:32; 19:9
but the rigid exclusion of any other reason for divorce. In that respect
Paul's teaching in verses 10 and 11 is thoroughly in line with our Lord's
teaching and this is directly affirmed in the expression, "Not I but the
Lord". All that is being claimed here is that our Lord's provision *for the
case of adultery* is not within the universe of discourse in verses 10 and 11.
Later on we shall have occasion to stress the parallelism between Paul's
teaching in verses 10 and 11 and our Lord's teaching in the synoptic
Gospels.

[3] The difficulty of determining the exact force of the verb $\dot{\alpha}\phi\acute{\iota}\eta\mu\iota$ in
verses 11, 12, and 13 is very great indeed. Commentators and translators
vary considerably in their judgment. There are three distinct renderings:
"leave" or "part from", "put away", and "divorce". To give examples
from English Versions: The Authorised Version (1611) renders by "put
away" in verses 11 and 12 and by "leave" in verse 13; the English Revised

prohibition rests upon the same principle as that upon which
our Lord's own teaching rests — man and wife are one flesh,
and what God has joined together let not man put asunder

(1881) by "leave" in each case, as also the American Revised (1901); the
Revised Standard (1946) by "divorce" in all three cases; the Roman
Catholic Revision of the Challoner-Rheims Version (1941) by "put away"
in each case; R. A. Knox (Roman Catholic, 1944) by "put away" in
verses 11 and 12 and by "part with" in verse 13.

It seems to the present writer that the rendering "divorce" is hardly
warranted. If the word, "divorce" is used in the same sense as "put away",
then all that could be urged in support of this latter rendering could be
pleaded in support of the rendering "divorce". But in an instance of this
kind the word "divorce" is very liable to convey to English readers the
notion of dissolution of the marriage bond. And there does not appear to
be warrant for supposing that the verb ἀφίημι, as used by Paul in these
verses, carries such force. Hence the Revised Standard Version (1946)
does not appear to have good ground for rendering the word thus. The
reasons for this judgment will become apparent as we proceed.

The crux of the difficulty inheres in the decision between the renderings
"put away" and "leave" (in the sense of "part from"). The verb ἀφίημι
has a great variety of meanings in the New Testament. With all these
shades of meaning we are not now directly concerned. The question is:
is it used in these verses in the sense of "put away" or in the sense of
"leave" or "part from"? Abundant instances of the latter sense could be
cited, but this meaning is so frequent and indisputable that citation is
unnecessary. On the other hand, there are very few instances where the
sense of "put away" is tenable. At the utmost there seem to be only
four — Matt. 13:36; 27:50; Mark 4:36; 15:37. Matthew 13:36; Mark
4:36 — ἀφεὶς τοὺς ὄχλους and ἀφέντες τὸν ὄχλον respectively —
have reference to parting with the multitude of the people. It is apparent
that the notion of sending away the people is quite appropriate; in both
cases this idea is possible and makes good sense. But with reference to
such a rendering the following observations should be made.

(a) Even if we regard the notion of "sending away" as correct and
attach to the notion the most formal character of dismissal, it can readily
be detected that dismissal of this sort hardly rises to the strength of
"putting away".

(b) The verb does not necessarily imply, however, "formal dismissal".
As Moulton and Milligan point out, "it may just as well mean simply 'let
go,' as in ordinary colloquial speech" (*The Vocabulary of the Greek Testament*, London, 1930, p. 97).

(c) The meaning "leave" is just as appropriate as is that of "dismissing".

In these two instances therefore the meaning is not necessarily "send
away", and even if this is the meaning the rendering "put away" is too
strong.

In Matthew 27:50 — Ἰησοῦς ... ἀφῆκεν τὸ πνεῦμα — the idea of

(Matt. 19:4–6; Mark 10:6–9). The parenthetical clauses —
"but if she does depart, let her remain unmarried or be
reconciled to her husband" — do not relax the stringency of

"leaving" is again possible. "Let go" or "release" is also quite possible.
But the notion of "dismissing" or "sending forth" is the most appropriate.
In Mark 15:37 — 'Ιησοῦς ἀφεὶς φωνὴν μεγάλην ἐξέπνευσεν — the
meaning "send forth" is entirely feasible. But again the thought of "letting go" in the sense of "letting out" is also possible (cf. LXX Genesis 45:2
where ἀφίημι translates the Hebrew נָתַן).

We see therefore that there is very little evidence in the usage of the
New Testament for the rendering "send away". There is no instance
where this import is absolutely required. Even when this rendering is
quite appropriate the import is distinctly weaker than that of our English
expression "put away".

In the LXX there are a few instances where ἀφίημι translates the Hebrew שָׁלַח and where the meaning is distinctly "send away" — Leviticus
16:10; Job 39:5. In Genesis 35:18 this verb translates the Hebrew יָצָא and
means "to depart". In the LXX generally, however, ἀφίημι means "to
leave", "to suffer" (permit), "to let go".

It is not without significance that ἀφίημι is used in the Gospels with
reference to the forsaking of all to follow Christ (cf. Matt. 19:29; Mark
10:29, 30; Luke 18:28, 29). In Luke 18:29 the expression ἀφῆκεν γυναῖκα
occurs in this connection. The thought is distinctly that of "leaving" or
"parting from" rather than that of "sending away".

Finally, a word may be said about the numerous instances in both
Testaments in which ἀφίημι is used with reference to the remission of
sins. If the underlying notion in remission is that of putting away sin,
then abundant support for this notion of "putting away" could be derived from this usage. But it is not by any means apparent that this is
the underlying notion. It appears to be rather that of "letting go", "waiv-
ing", with the result that the person is relieved or released from his sins.

For the foregoing reasons ἀφίημι has been rendered by the word "leave"
in the translation given in the discussion. It is fully recognised, of course,
that the rendering "send away" is possible and that the legitimacy of such
a rendering cannot be conclusively denied. In at least one instance in
classical Greek the verb has this force in reference to marriage (Herodotus:
History, V, 39 — τὴν ἔχει γυναῖκα . . . ταύτην ἀπέντα, ἄλλην ἐσαγ-
αγέσθαι). Yet it cannot be established that this is the force of the word
in the Scripture passage concerned. On the other hand, ἀφίημι must at
least carry the strength of the word "leave". This rendering is in accord
with the preponderant usage in the New Testament as well as in the LXX.
The meaning of Paul here seems to be most precisely conveyed by such
English expressions as "part from", "separate from", "let go". If this
weaker force of the verb is recognised and adopted, this only serves to
strengthen Paul's injunction in these verses. It is not simply that Paul
prohibits "putting away" or "divorce" in these conditions. He prohibits

the injunction; they do not have the effect of according any right or liberty to separate oneself or to put away. In other words, the parenthesis does not express an exception to the *law* enunciated in the prohibition itself. In this respect the parenthesis has a very different force from the exceptive clause in Matthew 5:32; 19:9. There the exceptive clause expresses an exception to the *wrong* of putting away; for the cause of fornication a man has the right to put away his wife. But here, in the situation envisaged by the apostle, the woman is not given the *right* to separate herself nor the man the *right* to leave or to put away. Paul is not saying, "Let not one spouse leave the other except under the following circumstance". This manifest difference between I Corinthians 7:11 and Matthew 5:32; 19:9 shows again, in another respect, the impropriety of appealing to this text in support of the right to put away for the cause of fornication. That right is established by Matthew 5:32; 19:9. But this right receives no confirmation nor do the nature and effect of the exercise of this right receive any elucidation from I Corinthians 7:11. The reason is simply that in Matthew the exceptive clause propounds a right which is the one exception to the wrong of putting away; in I Corinthians 7:11 no *right* of separation or dismissal is propounded. Hence any appeal to I Corinthians 7:11 to defend the *right* of separation without the right of dissolution is a distortion of the apostle's teaching.[4]

What then is the force of the parenthetical clauses? The answer should be apparent. Paul recognises that human nature is perverse, that even Christians act perversely and notwithstanding the wrong of separation or dismissal the parties to marriage may violate right and perpetrate wrong.

even the departure of the believing spouse. The prohibition, therefore, of even the least drastic form of separation emphasises all the more the wrong of the more drastic forms, namely, "putting away" or "divorce". It can be seen, therefore, that a profound ethical interest may be bound up with the proper assessment of the force of ἀφίημι as used here by Paul. It is not merely "divorce" that Paul prohibits in these cases but also what might appear to be an innocuous form of simple separation.

⁴ What is being controverted here again is the position taken by Roman Catholics and others that I Corinthians 7:10, 11 supports the conclusion that Matthew 5:32; 19:9 enunciate the right of separation from bed and board but not the right to dissolve the bond of marriage.

It is for that evil contingency that the parenthesis provides —
"but if she actually does depart, let her remain unmarried or
be reconciled to her husband". He is saying in effect, "If
separation has actually taken place, then certain provisions
must be adhered to. Let the breach be healed. Failing that,
under no conditions may another marriage be undertaken."
In other words, the parenthesis simply regulates the wrong
when it has taken place but does not in the least legitimate
the separation itself.[5]

In verse 12 Paul passes on to deal with an entirely different
situation. In the preceding verses he dealt with marriages in
which both spouses are Christian. In verse 12 he proceeds to
deal with what we may call mixed marriages. This is indicated
by the phrase, τοῖς δὲ λοιποῖς (that is, those who are in the
remaining case not dealt with hitherto), by the emphasis
upon the first personal pronoun, ἐγώ, and by the words,
οὐκ ὁ Κύριος (not the Lord). The emphasis upon the first
personal pronoun and the addition of the negative, "not the
Lord" draw our attention to the distinction between the
injunctions of this passage, as written in the exercise of
apostolic authority and inspiration, and the injunctions of
verses 10 and 11 which were written not only in the exercise
of apostolic authority but for which Paul could also plead
the authority of the Lord's own teaching. When Paul says,
"I, not the Lord" he is not drawing a distinction between
inspired and authoritative statements, on the one hand, and
his own uninspired judgment, on the other. Such a supposition
is contradicted by the very terms Paul uses and by the mandatory manner in which he enjoins the regulations. In verse 17,
for example, he says, "And so ordain I in all the churches".
It would have been not only presumption but logical contra-

---

[5] The question might well be raised: are there not some aggravated
circumstances under which it may be legitimate for one spouse to leave
the other? All that can be said here is that this text cannot properly be
construed as enunciating any such liberty. In view of the emphasis and
sanction by which the prohibition of separation is enforced in verses 10
and 11b, the parenthesis may not be interpreted as making provision for
the legitimacy of separation under certain supposed conditions.

diction for Paul to say, "So ordain I in all the churches" if in verse 12 he is drawing a sharp distinction between the authoritative decision of the Lord and his own merely human opinion. The distinction is rather between teaching that was expressly given by Christ in the days of his flesh and the teaching that did not come within the compass of Christ's own deliverances while upon earth. He is saying in effect, "I am now going to deal with cases on which the Lord himself did not give a verdict". But he is proceeding to do so as one who had received mercy of the Lord to be faithful (vs. 25), as one who had the Spirit of God (vs. 40), and as one who could protest, in the exercise of his apostolic authority, "If any one thinks he is a prophet or Spiritual, let him acknowledge that the things which I write to you are the commandment of the Lord" (I Cor. 14:37).

The cases with which Paul is now dealing are those in which one of the spouses is a Christian and the other is an unbeliever. He is not dealing, of course, with the entrance upon such an anomalous relationship. In verse 39 the words, "only in the Lord" show that for Paul entrance upon such a marital relationship is contrary to the Christian profession. Neither are we to suppose that Paul is dealing with the case of the believer who, contrary to Christian principle, entered into such a marital relation and then *de facto* finds himself or herself in the anomalous situation. The principles Paul sets forth will, of course, apply to such a case, but apparently that is not the precise situation that the apostle has in view. It is rather certain that what Paul has in mind is the case of those who were married as unbelievers, and that after marriage one of the spouses became a Christian. The convert now finds himself or herself in a mixed marital relation.

We can readily imagine what heart-burning this question must have evoked in the early church. What is to be done in such a case? the early converts must have asked. Will not the believer be contaminated and compromised by such an anomalous relationship? How can a believer be one flesh with an unbeliever? And what about the offspring? Will not the children contract defilement from the unbelieving partner? Such questions would inevitably have harassed the minds and

consciences of sensitive but uninstructed believers. It is to
such a perplexed state of mind that Paul directs his apostolic
teaching.

The answer of the apostle is decisive and unambiguous.
In such cases the marriage union is inviolate and must be
regarded as such. The believing partner must not take any
initiative in leaving or sending away the unbeliever. "If any
brother has an unbelieving wife, and she is pleased to dwell
with him, let him not leave her. And a wife who has an
unbelieving husband, and he is pleased to dwell with her, let
her not leave her husband" (vss. 12, 13). It is noteworthy that
the initiative in the separation is in both cases contemplated
as the action taken by the believer and is not here envisaged
as action taken by the unbeliever. We should not, however,
suppose that the unbeliever could not be conceived of in the
situation as leaving or as sending away the believer. There
would not appear to be any warrant for supposing that civil
jurisprudence in the Roman world of the time accorded to the
Christian any peculiar advantage in this respect. It was not
necessary for the apostle to mention all the possibilities and
eventualities; his insertion of the clause in both cases, "and
she (or he) is content to dwell with him (or her)" is intended
to cover various eventualities in the matter of the will of the
unbeliever. It was sufficient for the apostle to direct his
instructions to the believer in the case and prescribe that in
no event was the believer to take the initiative in effecting a
separation.

Verse 14 gives the reason why the believing spouse is not
to part from or send away the unbeliever. "For the unbelieving husband is sanctified in the wife, and the unbelieving
wife is sanctified in the brother: else were your children
unclean, but now are they holy." We should not infer that
Paul here intended to state the whole reason why separation
should not be resorted to. The most basic reason that must
have been presupposed in all of the apostle's reasoning is that,
by divine ordinance, man and wife are one flesh and what God
has joined together man should not put asunder. Here, however, Paul adduces as the reason for maintaining the union
that consideration which is most directly pertinent to the
fears entertained by the Corinthian converts and, in so doing,
he enunciates the great principle that would for ever silence

suspicion of defilement or compromise in the circumstance contemplated. All objection and scruple in this matter must be laid aside by the consideration that the unbelieving spouse is sanctified in the believer.

In this we have a very striking disclosure respecting the implications of the Christian faith. It is far from being the case that the believer contracts defilement from the unbeliever; the reverse is rather the case. The unbeliever contracts sanctification from the believer. Nothing less than this is the import of the apostle's deliverance. There are the following observations that should be mentioned.

(1) This principle evinces the potency of the Christian faith.

(2) It discloses to us something of the way in which the covenant principle or relationship operates in the Christian economy.

(3) The marriage relation, when sanctified by the Christian faith of even one spouse, has certain soteric implications; God honours and blesses the marriage institution as a channel for the conveyance of sanctifying grace. Through marriage the forces of redemptive grace are brought to bear in some way upon unbelievers.

It should be recognised that the sanctification of which Paul here speaks cannot be the sanctification of regeneration and actual salvation. He is certainly not propounding the position that marriage is a sacrament of saving grace and works *ex opere operato*. Not even a Romanist would claim that. It is rather assumed that one of the spouses is an unbeliever and therefore outside the pale of actual salvation. The sanctification of which Paul speaks, therefore, must be the sanctification of privilege, connection and relationship. This fact, however, should not lead us to depreciate the significance of the kind of sanctification expressed. Though not tantamount to actual salvation, this sanctification is, nevertheless, beneficent and gracious in character; it is a blessing accruing from the grace resident in the covenant or representative principle. And though this blessing does not in and of itself bring salvation, yet it places the person who is the beneficiary of it in the channel of saving grace, in a position of close proximity to the saving grace of God and therefore in a position of peculiar advantage. Marriage, in the situation presupposed, may be regarded as an avenue along which the means of grace travel.

Though the due recognition and appreciation of this grace do not in the least provide encouragement to believers to marry unbelievers (marriage is not to be adopted as a method of evangelisation), and though believers should marry only in the Lord, nevertheless the believer who actually finds himself in a mixed marital relationship is given the assurance that grace is more potent than nature, that greater is He who is in the believer than he that is in the world.

Additional corroboration is given to this principle by Paul's appeal to the sanctification of the offspring — "else were your children unclean, but now are they holy". The children of one believing parent receive sanctification from the believing spouse rather than defilement from the unbelieving. Believing spouses, in the situation envisaged, might hesitate to cooperate with unbelieving partners in the procreation of children on the suspicion that the children would contract defilement from the unbeliever. Paul says, in effect, "Let there be no hesitancy in discharging the conjugal debt in such cases and in obeying the divine command to be fruitful and multiply; the children are sanctified in one believing parent". Again we see the triumph of grace over the corruption of nature. As far as the privilege here spoken of is concerned, the children of one believing parent are in the same position as the children of parents who are both believers. The representative principle follows the line of the covenant of grace, exemplified in the believer, rather than the line of the covenant of works, exemplified in the unbeliever; the solidarity is unto life rather than unto death.

We thus see with what gracious, divine provisions the sanctity and inviolability of the marriage institution is guarded and supported even in the anomalous circumstance where a believer and unbeliever are joined together in this estate. In the teaching of Scripture nothing is clearer than the deep-seated cleavage that exists between the children of light and the children of darkness. How severe is the Pauline warning against being unequally yoked with unbelievers (II Cor. 6:14–18). And it might well appear that the intimacy of the marital bond brought believers and unbelievers into such close union with one another that the proper interests of holiness could be preserved only by separation or even dissolution, when it is found that the one spouse is a child of light and the other a child of darkness. It is precisely here that the sacredness of the marriage bond is attested; the very cleavage between faith and unbelief constitutes no ground for separation or dissolution. And we are reminded thereby that marriage is also a physical union — "the two shall be one flesh". For that reason the lack of the deepest moral and spiritual affinity does not dissolve it, nor does the presence of the most profound spiritual incompatibility provide, of itself, any valid ground for its dissolution. In this passage Paul indeed acknowledges that he is not able to plead the authority of teaching given by the Lord himself in the days of his flesh — "I say, not the Lord". He is speaking exclusively in terms of his apostolic inspiration and commission. But we can discern in this very emphasis of his the undercurrent of harmony between his teaching and that of the Lord himself. Jesus did not allow divorce for spiritual cleavage or incompatibility. And the one exception our Lord sanctioned, to the exclusion of every other, most eloquently advertises the agreement of Paul's verdict here with the principle so unequivocally established by our Lord's utterances.

In verses 12 and 13 we found that Paul very strictly enjoins upon the believer, in the case of a mixed marriage, not to leave or put away the unbeliever. The burden of his injunction is directed of necessity, therefore, to the believer. But the believer is not the only party to this union, and so the will of the unbeliever cannot be entirely ignored or discounted. It is for this reason that Paul added in each case the condition respecting the will of the unbeliever, namely, "and he (or she) be pleased to dwell with her (or him)". Paul here distinctly allows for the possibility that the unbeliever may not be pleased to remain. Perchance the religious discordance may be so intense that the unbeliever is constrained to depart; or some other reason may dispose to such action. What is to happen in such an event? It is here that the significance of

I Corinthians 7:15 appears: "But if the unbeliever depart, let him depart: the brother or the sister is not bound in such cases".

It should be noted that there is a striking decisiveness and even severity about Paul's judgment in this eventuality. In verses 12 and 13 Paul is very decisive that the believer should not leave or send away the unbeliever in a case of mixed marriage; he uses the imperative in both instances ($\mu\grave{\eta}$ $\mathring{\alpha}\phi\iota\acute{\epsilon}\tau\omega$). This imperative is distinctly mandatory. In verse 15 we find an imperative also ($\chi\omega\rho\iota\zeta\acute{\epsilon}\sigma\theta\omega$). In this instance the imperative is permissive and in that respect has a slightly different force from the imperatives of verses 12 and 13.[6] It is not a command to the unbelieving spouse to separate himself or herself. The unbelieving spouse is regarded rather as in the process of wilful separation or as having wilfully departed, and the departure is viewed as initiated or as accomplished when the action or attitude denoted by the imperative is to take effect. We have here an eloquent distinction and emphasis; the imperative, "let him depart", has bearing not so much upon the unbelieving spouse, who is deserting or has deserted, as upon the believing spouse who has been deserted. It is not a command to the unbeliever to depart; it is not even a concession to the unbeliever of the right to depart; it enunciates, rather, the liberty that is granted to, and the attitude that is to be assumed by, the believer in this event, and is, in effect, "let the unbeliever be gone".[7] It prepares for the statement which immediately follows: "the brother or the sister is not bound in such cases".

As has been indicated, there is both decisiveness and severity in the injunction, "let him depart". If the unbeliever wilfully departs, let separation take its course, let it become an accomplished fact; the believer is not under any obligation to pursue the deserting spouse and is freed from all marital debts

---

[6] Cf. Winer: A Grammar of the Idiom of the New Testament, § 43; Blass: Grammar of New Testament Greek, § 67; Moulton: A Grammar of New Testament Greek (Edinburgh, 1930), Vol. I, p. 172; A. T. Robertson: A New Short Grammar of the Greek Testament, § 407.

[7] Cf. T. C. Edwards: A Commentary on the First Epistle to the Corinthians (New York, 1886), p. 174; R. C. H. Lenski: First Epistle to the Corinthians (Columbus, 1935), p. 299.

and duties. Here is decisiveness. But there is also the note
of severity, not indeed with respect to the deserted believer
but with reference to the deserting unbeliever, and may be
rendered in the legitimate paraphrase, "let him be gone".
The harshness and terseness of the expression bespeak the
severity of the judgment passed upon the deserting spouse
and indicate the absence of any further obligation in the matter
of conjugal dues.

   This introduces us to one of the most perplexing questions
in New Testament interpretation. It is the question of the
exact force of the verb, "is not bound" (οὐ δεδούλωται).
That it means separation from bed and board (*a thoro et
mensa*) and that the deserted believer is not under obligation
to discharge marital functions and debts to the deserting
spouse is quite obvious; it cannot mean anything less. But
the question is whether it also implies more, namely, the
dissolution of the marriage bond and liberty for the believer
to marry another. In other words, does desertion in such a
case have virtually the same effect as adultery and give
to the innocent partner the right of divorce and liberty to
remarry?
   On the supposition that this latter interpretation is correct
and that here the right of divorce and remarriage is accorded,
one of the most important aspects of the whole question is:
how can such an interpretation be compatible with Matthew
5:32; 19:9? Our Lord, as found already, allows only one
reason for which a man may put away his wife; his pronouncements leave no room for doubt that adultery is the only cause.
But if, in the circumstance with which we are now dealing,
the believer deserted may remarry, is there not another reason
for which marriage may be dissolved? And how can the
Pauline teaching be reconciled with the Lord's teaching,
especially since Paul himself must be regarded as alluding to
that teaching when he says in verse 10, 'But to the married
I give charge, not I, but the Lord"? It is this difficulty that
has led many to take the position that the conflict that would
be instituted between Paul and our Lord himself excludes the
possibility of interpreting I Corinthians 7:15 in terms of a
dissolution of the marriage bond. And so the liberty granted

by Paul, it is claimed, cannot be greater than that of separation from bed and board.

This position needs to be carefully examined, and the question must be faced: is the conflict alleged in such a position real? Would the view that I Corinthians 7:15 contemplates dissolution of the marriage bring Paul into conflict with Christ's own deliverances? It is the conviction of the present writer that this is not necessarily the case and that for the following reasons.

1. Jesus was dealing with the question of "putting away". Paul is not dealing with putting away but with wilful desertion on the part of the unbeliever. Paul is most explicit that the believer is not to put away the unbeliever; in that respect he is as emphatic as our Lord himself. Dissonance in the matter of faith gives no ground for divorce. But wilful "going away" on the part of the unbeliever introduces a new situation. The distinction must be duly appreciated. The two cases are in different categories and so the principle clearly established by our Lord's utterances, and by implication reiterated in this passage by Paul himself, cannot without question be regarded as applying to the contingency that is viewed as existing in verse 15. In a word, the believer does not "put away" the unbeliever; he or she is required not to do that; the unbeliever "goes away" of his or her own accord.

2. Paul is obviously dealing from verse 12 onwards with cases that did not come within the purview of our Lord's teaching. This is clearly asserted in the words by which this passage is introduced, "But to the rest I say, not the Lord". This difference should caution us and should constrain us to hesitate, at least, before concluding that what our Lord said with reference to that which came within his purview has the same direct relevance to what Paul says with respect to a very different situation.

3. It is a feasible assumption that our Lord was dealing with cases in which both spouses are believers by profession and covenant relationship. This assumption is confirmed by what Paul says in this chapter in verses 10 and 11. For Paul is there dealing with the cases in which both spouses are believers and it is in reference to such a case that he appeals to the authority of Christ.

4. There is a striking difference between the terms Paul uses and the injunctions he gives in verses 10 and 11, when the separation of two believing spouses is in view, and the terms and injunctions of verse 15, when desertion on the part of an unbeliever is envisaged. This patent distinction must be fully appreciated. In the former case he strictly enjoins that if separation has taken place the spouse who has separated must remain unmarried or be reconciled. The thought could properly be paraphrased as follows: "Be reconciled, restore normal and harmonious marital relations, but in no case may another marriage be contracted". In the latter case — that concerned with the deserting unbeliever — the change is surely most significant. There is no injunction to remain unmarried. There is no *obviously* implied exhortation to remain unmarried. Instead, Paul says in respect of the deserting spouse, "Let him (or her) depart", an expression symptomatic of finality, as if he should say, "Let this be a closed case and let separation take its course". Finally, he asserts that the deserted spouse is not bound. These striking differences demonstrate a radical difference of issue and effect in the two cases. It is when this difference is duly appreciated that the bearing of Paul's appeal to the authority of our Lord's teaching in the one case and of his disavowal of any such appeal in the other case takes on significance. Since our Lord's statements fell into the category of the case dealt with in verses 10 and 11 and not into the category of the case dealt with in verse 15, and since there is such a radical difference between the issue and effect of the separation of verse 11 and the desertion of verse 15, it would be distinctly precarious, if not indefensible, to take our Lord's words and apply them to a case that is so entirely different and that did not come, as Paul explicitly states, within the purview of his teaching. In other words, the outcome and the ensuing obligations of the situation contemplated in verse 15 are so different from the outcome and ensuing obligations of the case with which our Lord's teaching was concerned that, to say the least, we must refrain from dogmatism to the effect that our Lord's unambiguous exclusion of every reason for *divorce* except adultery necessarily excludes the dissolution of the marriage bond in the case of desertion by an unbelieving partner. It is quite apparent that the pivot on which the

difference in Paul's verdict turns is desertion of a believer by an unbeliever. It is this circumstance that draws to itself such far-reaching significance and defines the line of distinction. Paul's emphasis should caution us not to suppress or discount this factor.

For these reasons we may conclude that if the expression, "is not bound" (οὐ δεδούλωται) in verse 15 should prove to bear the import, "is released from the bond of marriage", such an interpretation should not be regarded as in conflict with our Lord's teaching in Matthew 5:32; 19:9; Mark 10:11; Luke 16:18, and that we should not approach this exegetical question on the assumption that this interpretation is excluded by reason of the contradiction that it would involve between the teaching of Jesus and the teaching of Paul.[8]

In dealing with the interpretation of οὐ δεδούλωται we shall consider first the arguments in favour of the weaker force, namely, that simply of separation from bed and board.

(1) The verb used can be interpreted as freedom from another bondage than that of release from the marriage bond. A person who is under obligation to perform the marital duties connected with bed and board is certainly "bound"; there is a tie that binds to the discharge of such functions. If a deserted partner were under obligation to furnish alimony to the deserting spouse that would be a still more burdensome bondage. And most grievous of all would be the obligation to pursue the deserting spouse and under such conditions endeavour, as best he or she could, to fulfil marital functions. We can readily see the strength that would attach to the idea of being "bound" if a deserted believer were under such obligations and how significant the release from all such obligation would be. Since liberty no less than this is implied in the terms Paul uses and since such liberty is of sufficient significance to satisfy the verb οὐ δεδούλωται, may it not be unwarranted to put any additional import into the word?

---

[8] The Romish Church, while denying that the exceptive clause of Matthew 19:9 allows anything more than separation from bed and board, nevertheless admits that I Corinthians 7:15 deals with a case where marriage, even though consummated, may be dissolved (*cf.* Arthur Devine: *op. cit.*, pp. 86 ff.; *A Commentary on the New Testament*, as cited above, p. 460; Aug. Lehmkuhl: *op. cit.*, p. 60).

(2) Since the force outlined above gives adequate meaning to the term in question, is it not precarious to go farther and posit a much stronger meaning when the issue at stake is so important and far-reaching? While granting that the stronger force is possible or even probable, is it not precarious to make an issue that concerns the dissolution of the marriage bond to rest upon so slim a basis? May we properly base such a weighty conclusion upon what is simply a possible or probable interpretation?

(3) If we suppose that οὐ δεδούλωται has reference to the dissolution of the marriage bond, would not Paul be setting up a double standard of ethics, one for the case where two believers are concerned and the other for the case where an unbeliever enters into the situation? In the former case all thought of dissolution is excluded. Does the fact that an unbeliever is involved in the latter case alter in any way the sanctity of the marriage bond? The marriage is valid and sacred in both cases and surely the norms which guard the validity are the same.

On the basis of such considerations as these it is difficult to make out a strong or valid case for the view that οὐ δεδού-λωται means dissolution. Nevertheless on this side of the question there are also cogent arguments. To these we may now turn.[9]

(1) There is the striking difference between verse 11, where Paul deals with the separation of two believing spouses, and

[9] As representative of a great deal of Protestant interpretation the comments of Calvin on verses 12 and 13 may here be quoted. "Reliquos vocat, in quibus locum habet exceptis, quominus subiiciantur communi aliorum legi: nam coniugium inaequale diversam habet rationem, dum coniuges religione inter se differunt. Duobus autem membris hanc quaestionem absolvit: prius est, fidelem non debere ab infideli discedere, nec quaerere divortium, nisi repudietur: secundum est, si infidelis coniugem religionis causa repudiet, fratrem aut sororem liberari a vinculo coniugii per tale repudium . . . Repugnantia autem nulla est cum superioribus: nam quum religio ac sanctitas fidei coniugalis a Deo pendeat, quae necessitudo amplius mulieri piae restat cum infideli marito, postquam Dei odio eiecta est? . . . Hoc secundum est membrum, in quo liberat fidelem virum, qui paratus habitare cum uxore impia respuitur, et similiter mulierem quae non sua culpa repudiatur a viro: nam tunc infidelis divortium magis cum Deo quam cum homine coniugem facit. Est igitur hic peculiaris ratio, quia non modo solvitur, sed abrumpitur primum et praecipuum vinculum."

verse 15, where he deals with desertion on the part of an unbeliever. The weaker import of οὐ δεδούλωται would apply to the separation contemplated in verse 11; as long as the separation is in effect the partner deserted would not be under obligations to bed and board. Now, if freedom from obligations to bed and board is all that Paul has in mind in verse 15 we should expect him to say virtually the same thing in verse 15 as he says in verse 11. But that is precisely what he does not say. In verse 15 we find a terseness and severity of terms which, viewed from the standpoint of the separation envisioned, are indicative of decisiveness and finality — "let him (or her) depart", that is, "let him (or her) be gone". Consequently we are led to expect that Paul had much more in mind in verse 15, and with reference to the separation in view there, than is expressed or implied in verse 11. But if he has much more in mind than the separation from bed and board of verse 11, what is this "plus"? Apparently the only direction from which we can derive any additional liberty for the deserted partner is that of liberty from the marital bond itself. In other words, the only "plus" that can explain the difference between the issue in verse 11 and the issue in verse 15 is the "plus" of freedom from the bond of marriage.[10]

(2) In this same chapter in verses 27 and 39, as also in Romans 7:2, Paul speaks of the bond of marriage and, in connection with such, uses the verb δέω. Verse 39 supplies a good example: "A wife is bound for so long a time as her husband lives" (γυνὴ δέδεται ἐφ' ὅσον χρόνον ζῇ ὁ ἀνὴρ αὐτῆς). If δέδεται has reference to the bond of marriage, οὐ δέδεται would certainly indicate the opposite, namely, freedom from such a bond. Now, it must be said that δέω

[10] It might be argued that the additional element implied in verse 15 as over against verse 11 is that in verse 15 the separation from bed and board is regarded as permanent without any hope of reconciliation, whereas in verse 11 the separation can never properly be regarded as permanent. There is undoubtedly this difference, and a good argument can be made out in support of the contention that this supplies the "plus" required. A full discussion of this contention cannot be offered now. Suffice it for the present to present the judgment that the *right* of permanent separation carries with it the *right* of dissolution, that a person may not rightfully regard himself as permanently separated from his spouse unless the marriage has been dissolved.

is not a stronger word than δουλόω, the verb used in verse 15. If anything, δουλόω is the stronger word. And so there is no reason why δεδούλωται should not perform the same service as δέδεται in reference to the marital bond. Consequently οὐ δεδούλωται, as the opposite of δεδούλωται, would indicate the negative of the bond of marriage and would naturally suggest freedom from that bond. So it can with good and rather cogent reason be argued that οὐ δεδούλωται[11] in verse 15 means, "is not bound in marriage".

(3) The force of the objection urged above in support of the weaker interpretation of οὐ δεδούλωται, namely, that Paul would be setting up a dual standard of ethics with respect to the marital tie, can be offset if we properly estimate the unbelieving and obstinate state of mind of the deserting unbeliever and the character of the sin entailed in this kind of desertion. We must also take into account the presupposed impossibility of bringing considerations and motives arising from the Christian faith to bear upon the unbeliever in such a case. In this connection we must remember that, in respect of adultery, it is the character of the sin that makes it the legitimate ground of divorce. The marriage tie is in itself just as sacred in the case where one spouse commits adultery. In fact, it is because of the sanctity of the bond that this sin is so grievous. But the innocent party is nevertheless at liberty to dissolve the marital tie. This does not mean that there is any impairment of the sanctity of marriage as such, nor does it imply any interference with the ethics which guard and govern that sanctity. The case is rather that so heinous has been the desecration of this sanctity that the marriage bond may properly be dissolved. So in this case of wilful and determined desertion on the part of an unbeliever the circumstances of the desertion and the obduracy of the person concerned may feasibly be considered as providing proper ground for dissolution without having to suppose that a dual standard of ethics is thereby posited. The infidelity of the deserting party may so condition the complexion of the act of desertion that, like adultery, it provides proper ground for releasing the Christian spouse from the marital bond.

[11] The use of the perfect tense should not be overlooked; it contemplates a condition resultant upon a past action.

For these reasons there is much to be said in favour of the
view that I Corinthians 7:15 contemplates the dissolution of
the bond of marriage. This interpretation must not be sum-
marily dismissed as inconsistent with our Lord's teaching or
as incompatible with the ethics of marriage as enunciated by
Paul himself.[12]

It is, however, of the greatest importance to maintain that,
if this position is adopted, the application of this liberty must
be limited to the precise conditions specified or implied by the
apostle.[13] Too frequently this liberty has been applied to cases

[12] It might be argued that although I Corinthians 7:15 has dissolution
of the marriage bond in view, yet this does not imply the right of remarriage on the part of the parties involved. This again is a question that
would require some detailed discussion. Suffice it to say at present that
the notion of dissolution without the right of remarriage, at least on the
part of the innocent spouse, does not appear tenable.

[13] The statement of the Westminster Confession of Faith calls for some
comment. In the chapter entitled, "Of Marriage, and Divorce" (chap.
XXIV), section VI reads as follows: "Although the corruption of man be
such as is apt to study arguments unduly to put asunder those whom God
hath joined together in marriage: yet, nothing but adultery, or such wilful
desertion as can no way be remedied by the Church, or civil magistrate,
is cause sufficient of dissolving the bond of marriage: wherein, a public
and orderly course of proceeding is to be observed; and the persons concerned in it not left to their own wills, and discretion, in their own case".
It is obvious that the Confession regards "such wilful desertion as can no
way be remedied by the Church, or civil magistrate" as a sufficient cause
for dissolution of the bond of marriage and of putting asunder those whom
God hath joined together in marriage. This position is based upon I Corinthians 7:15; it is the only proof text cited and, of course, it is the only
one that could reasonably be cited.

If I Corinthians 7:15 is to be interpreted as legitimating the dissolution
of the marriage bond in the circumstance contemplated, it may indeed be
conceded that cases may arise among professing Christians in which the
principle of I Corinthians 7:15 might apply. That is to say, a professing
Christian may exhibit such perversity in departing from his or her Christian spouse and show such opposition to the demands of the Christian
ethic that the desertion, in view of all the factors involved, may be regarded as abandonment of the Christian faith. In such an instance the
person deserting could be placed in the same category as an unbeliever
and desertion construed accordingly. In this situation I Corinthians 7:15
could be regarded as applicable and its provisions applied. If the Confession had such a situation in mind, as well as desertion by a professed unbeliever, when it used the description "such wilful desertion as can no way

that do not fall within the category defined by the context of I Corinthians 7:15. It is this loose and indiscriminating application that must be obviated. The following limitations must be observed.

(i) Paul is dealing with mixed marriages and not with marriage between two Christians. What he says in verse 15, therefore, cannot have relevance to a case of separation, however aggravated, where both spouses may be regarded, in the judgment of charity, as members of the household of faith. Such an application would be gross distortion of the text.

(ii) Paul is dealing with the case of wilful separation on the part of the unbeliever. He expressly disallows separation or dismissal on the part of the believer. The Christian must not take any initiative in parting from or in putting away the unbeliever. The believer may not even solicit desertion on the part of the unbeliever. To be very concrete, the believer must not make it so unbearable for the unbeliever that the latter will be induced or compelled to depart.

(iii) The separation in view must be conceived of as finding its root in fundamental religious discordance, not simply disagreement respecting certain aspects of Christian faith and practice but discordance between the Christian faith and its antithesis.

be remedied by the Church, or civil magistrate", then the position could be defended. But the Confession does not make clear that this is precisely the construction or application intended. In the first place, it does not restrict the right of dissolution to the case of desertion of a believer on the part of an unbeliever, and, secondly, in the case of separation of two professed believers, it does not restrict the right of dissolution to a case in which the deserting partner has, by the peculiarly perverse and aggravated nature of the desertion, put himself or herself in the same category as an unbeliever. Consequently it will have to be concluded that the proposition respecting wilful desertion in the Confession is not sufficiently guarded and delimited so as to confine itself to the teaching of the apostle in this passage. The Confession should not be blamed for all the loose thinking and practice which have appealed to it. The restrictions of the Confession are far-reaching when it says, "such wilful desertion as can no way be remedied by the Church, or civil magistrate". But the failure strictly to confine the liberty of dissolution to the precise conditions prescribed by the apostle in this passage must be recognised, and the loophole left thereby cannot be maintained on the basis of Scripture.

It is apparent, therefore, how unwarranted it is to apply this liberty to all wilful desertion. Not only does the immediate context of verse 15 demonstrate this but also verse 11. In the latter verse separation is undoubtedly in view and the possibility of its being permanent[14] is distinctly entertained. But in such a case there is the express provision, "let her remain unmarried or be reconciled to her husband", a provision that could not obtain if dissolution of the marriage were regarded as feasible. Hence, if we are to interpret I Corinthians 7:15 as legitimating dissolution of the bond of marriage, it is most necessary to restrict this liberty to conditions and circumstances which are analogous to those of the situation dealt with by the apostle. It is here that the gross abuse of this particular interpretation must be deplored and condemned. It is cause for lament that within the circle of professing believers desertion has been regarded as sufficient ground for divorce, and I Corinthians 7:15 has been wrested to do service in the defence of a cause that Paul never sanctioned.

Romans 7:1-3

In Romans 7:2, 3 Paul adduces the law respecting marriage as an illustration by which to commend to the understanding of his readers the doctrine respecting the effect of the death of Christ upon the relation of the believer to the law and to Christ. It is not necessary for the purpose now in view to discuss the rather difficult exegetical question involved in the similitude Paul uses. Those acquainted with the exegetical literature on these verses know how interpreters have laboured with the question of determining what, in the doctrine Paul is enunciating, is parallel to the death of the husband in the similitude instituted. The relevance of this passage to the question of divorce need not be perplexed, however, by that other exegetical question. The question we are concerned

---

[14] The word "permanent" is not used here in the sense that the parties to the separation may ever rightfully consider the separation as a *fait accompli* without any hope of reconciliation. They may never take the position that *finis* is written across their marital relations. The word "permanent" is used simply in the sense that reconciliation may never *de facto* be accomplished.

with now is simply the bearing of this passage upon the matter of divorce.

In reference to this precise question it is of importance to note that Paul is not dealing here expressly with the question of marriage and separation as he is in I Corinthians 7:10–15. The subject with which Paul is here dealing is the expansion and validation of what he had stated in Romans 6:14 — that sin does not have dominion over the believer, for he is not under law but under grace. The appeal to the law of marriage, specifically the law of marriage as it applies to the wife, is for the purpose of illustration. The death of the husband frees the wife from the law of her husband. So the death of Christ frees the believer from bondage to the law.

It is necessary to stress this only-too-obvious fact. While, on the one hand, we must not allow this consideration to obscure or rule out the significance of this passage as it bears upon the law of marriage, yet, on the other hand, we must not forget that the allusion to the law of marriage is incidental to Paul's main purpose. We must not fall into the mistake of loading his illustration with more significance than reasonably belongs to it in the context.

When Paul says in verse 1 that "the law has dominion over a man for so long a time as he lives"[15] we may properly regard him as intending to state a general principle. He is not referring specifically to the marriage law which in verses 2 and 3 is adduced as an example. Rather, the case is that he states the general principle in verse 1 and illustrates by a particular example in verses 2 and 3. He credits his readers at Rome with knowledge of that general principle and assumes that they will readily accede to its universal validity. The reason why he credits them with this knowledge and with ready acceptance is that they know the law.[16]

[15] ὁ νόμος κυριεύει τοῦ ἀνθρώπου ἐφ' ὅσον χρόνον ζῇ. It should be noted that this is generic. The use of ἄνθρωπος rather than ἀνήρ indicates that he is not suggesting the dominion of the law over the man as distinguished from the woman. It is the dominion of the law over humankind. In verses 2 and 3 he distinguishes between the man and the woman by the use of the distinguishing terms ἀνήρ and γυνή and applies the general principle of verse 1 to the marriage law as it governs the woman.

[16] The commentators have shown that Paul is not here distinguishing between those at Rome who knew the law and those who did not. All

This appeal to their knowledge of the law raises a question that has considerable relevance to our discussion. What is the law with the knowledge of which Paul credits his readers? It cannot reasonably be supposed that it is simply the general principle which he has just stated. Paul credits them, rather, with knowledge of the law in some more embracive sense and then, on that assumption, protests that their knowledge of that law should lead them readily to recognise the validity of the general principle, namely, that law has dominion over a man as long as he lives. When appeal is made in this way to knowledge of law there is one feasible conclusion, namely, that the law is the written law of the Old Testament, particularly the Mosaic law. Paul uses the word "law" ($\nu\acute{o}\mu os$) quite frequently in this sense (cf. 3:19; 5:13; I Cor. 9:8, 9; 14:21, 24; Gal. 3:10, 19), and there is no reason why we should look for the denotation in any other direction. Gentiles as well as Jews in the church at Rome could be credited with knowledge of the Old Testament and specifically with knowledge of the Mosaic law. So we may proceed on the assumption that this is the law Paul has in mind when he says, "for I speak to them who know the law".

This conclusion bears upon the force of the example Paul adduces in verses 2 and 3. If the Mosaic law is in view in verse 1 and if Paul proceeds with his argument on the assumption that his readers are acquainted with that law, we cannot but regard the very example which he adduces in verses 2 and 3 as in like manner elicited from, or at least borne out by, the Mosaic law.

We may not suppose, however, that such respect to the Mosaic law in any way weakens or curtails the validity and application of the law regarding marriage expressed in verses 2 and 3. The universal validity should be apparent for two reasons. (1) The general principle stated in verse 1 is one which Paul recognises as having unqualified validity, and surely the example by which he illustrates must have similar validity within its own specific sphere of operation. There

---

addressed are credited with this knowledge. The reasons for this conclusion need not be discussed here.

would have been a *non sequitur* in Paul's argument if the illustration did not exemplify in a particular case the application of the general principle. (2) If the illustration did not carry out the general principle, this failure would react fatally upon the doctrine being propounded. It is the example drawn from marriage that Paul uses to illustrate our bondage to the law and then our freedom from the law by the body of Christ. If the analogy in the marital sphere were not watertight, how would it fare for the doctrine which is Paul's main interest at this point? We must conclude, therefore, that the law respecting the bond of marriage referred to in verses 2 and 3, even though it is viewed as inherent in and elicited from the Mosaic law, is not for that reason impaired in respect of its universal validity and application.

The significance of this insistence needs to be stated and developed if we are to interpret aright the bearing of this passage on the subject of divorce. Since Paul states a principle of universal validity and application, a principle that applies to marriage as such, we are not to suppose that the law enunciated here is merely the law of marriage that applies within the pale of special revelation. Truly the Mosaic law was special revelation and Paul had that in mind when he adduced the law of marriage. But this fact must not be allowed to lead us to the fallacy, too frequently and oftentimes surreptitiously at work, that since appeal is made to special revelation this restricts the application of the principle to those who are the recipients and beneficiaries of that revelation. What Paul enunciates here is the basic law of marriage which applies to the institution wherever it exists, in other words, the law of Genesis 2:23, 24. Those who had the Mosaic law were indeed placed in a peculiarly advantageous position respecting the knowledge of that law. But the operation and obligation of the law are not restricted to the sphere in which it is thus known. The law binds wherever the institution exists, and is to the effect that the woman is bound by the law of her husband as long as he lives, that if while he lives she be married to another she will be called an adulteress but that when her husband dies she is free from that law and may be married to another.

This passage and the principle it embodies have been appealed to by Romish exegetes and theologians,[17] as well as by others who adopt a similar position, in support of the contention that marriage is indissoluble and that not even in the case of adultery may marriage be dissolved, although the spouses may, in this case, be separated *a toro et mensa*. In the preceding study of this question the position has been taken, particularly on the basis of Matthew 19:9, that marriage may be dissolved for the cause of adultery and in the event of such dissolution the innocent spouse is at liberty to contract another marriage. The question is now very acutely before us: how does such a position comport with what we have just found respecting the import of Romans 7:2, 3? How can we answer the argument of Rome and of Protestant theologians, such as those of the Church of England, that not even adultery is a proper ground for dissolution of the marriage bond (*divortium a vinculo matrimonii* as distinguished from *divortium a toro et mensa*)? For has not this text asserted very distinctly that it is death that frees from the bond of marriage and that the woman who is married to another while her husband lives shall be called an adulteress? The answer to this question will require a rather diffuse discussion.

The first observation to be made is that the appeal to this text on the part of the Romish Church, on the one hand, and other contentions and practices of Rome, on the other, are singularly incompatible. Since it is not claimed that similar inconsistency can be charged against the Church of England and its representatives, we shall focus attention on the Romish position. Though Rome vigorously contends for the indissolubility of the bond (*quoad vinculum*) of marriage she allows for the dissolution of unconsummated marriage between Christians in two events: (1) in the event of solemn profession of either party in a religious order and (2) in the event of papal

[17] *Cf*. Robert Bellarmine: "De Sacramento Matrimonii," Lib. I, Cap. XVI (*Disputationes*, Rome, 1838, Tom. 3, pp. 1148 ff.); Joseph Pohle: *The Sacraments: A Dogmatic Treatise* (St. Louis and London, 1937), Vol. IV, p. 192; Arthur Devine: *The Law of Christian Marriage* (New York, 1908), pp. 92 ff.; *A Commentary on the New Testament* (The Catholic Biblical Association, 1942), pp. 52 f.

dispensation.[18] Since in such cases the dissolution is *a vinculo* and not merely *a toro et mensa* and since, therefore, the marriage is dissolved, it follows that the party not making solemn profession in a religious order is at liberty to marry another and in the case of special papal dispensation both parties to the dissolution are at liberty to remarry. But how can such concessions be reconciled with Rome's appeal to Romans 7:2, 3 in support of the indissolubility of the marriage bond? If Romans 7:2, 3 allows for such exceptions, then the passage must be regarded as compatible with some exception and, consequently, cannot with propriety be quoted and cited in support of the proposition that *the only thing* that can dissolve the marriage bond is death.[19] For even on Rome's own assumptions Romans 7:2, 3 does admit of dissolution and of freedom to remarry in certain cases. In the precise terms of the passage itself, Rome allows that there are cases in which the woman may remarry while her first husband lives and yet not be branded as an adulteress. If this is so, how can Rome so easily appeal to Romans 7:2, 3 as supporting the doctrine of the indissolubility of the bond of marriage? Conceivably Rome might be quite consistent in maintaining her own peculiar doctrine of indissolubility and of the exceptions she allows in particular cases. What is being urged now is simply that she has fallen into inexcusable inconsistency when, in the defence of her own position and in opposition to dissolution on the ground of adultery, she appeals to Romans 7:2, 3 and then forthwith makes her own exceptions which as gravely impinge upon the principle asserted by Paul as does the exception in the case of adultery.[20] The upshot is that Rome has

---

[18] *Cf. Canons and Decrees of the Council of Trent*, Session XXIV, Canon 6; Bellarmine: *"De Monachis"*, Lib. II, Cap. XXXVIII (*op. cit.*, Tom. 2, pp. 405 ff.); *Synopsis Theologiae Dogmaticae* (New York, 1943), Tom. III, "De Paenitentia et Matrimonio", pp. 161 ff.; Joseph Pohle: *op. cit.*, pp. 201 ff.; Arthur Devine: *op. cit.*, pp. 89 ff.

[19] *Cf.* Joseph Pohle: *op. cit.*, p. 192.

[20] Though at this point we have spoken of divorce for adultery as an *exception* to Romans 7:2, 3, we are not to be understood as conceding that this is, strictly speaking, the proper construction or the most accurate terminology. We have used these terms at this point because we are conducting an *ad hominem* argument and do not wish to perplex the force

no right of appeal to Romans 7:2, 3 to disprove the right of
dissolution in the case of adultery as long as she herself
claims the legitimacy of dissolution in the case of solemn
profession in a religious order and in the case of papal dispensation unless she undertakes to present grounds for believing that Paul can well be regarded as envisaging the kind of
exception Rome posits but not the kind of exception which we
maintain. And this is an undertaking that Romish theologians
do not appear to fulfil.

It may be replied that, in arguing thus, sufficient account
has not been taken of the distinction which Rome draws
between unconsummated and consummated marriage. While
we are not disposed to suppress or discount the significance of
the conjugal act by which marriage is consummated, yet, as
far as the principle of Romans 7:2, 3 and its application are
concerned, what evidence do we possess from Scripture in
general or from Paul in particular to warrant the assumption
that a sharp line of distinction is to be drawn between consummated and unconsummated marriage? We can well understand how such a sharp line of distinction could be maintained
if it were held that unconsummated marriage is not really
marriage in terms of Romans 7:2, 3. In that event the principle
of Romans 7:2, 3 would apply only to consummated marriage
and would not come into operation until marriage is consummated by the conjugal act. On such a view Romans 7:2, 3
would have no relevance at all to unconsummated marriage.
But not even Rome takes that position.[21] Indeed, so far is this
from being the case that she is very jealous to restrict the
right of dissolution of unconsummated marriage between
Christians to the two exceptional cases of solemn profession in
a religious order and special papal dispensation. In all other
cases, according to Rome, the principle of Romans 7:2, 3

---

or point of the argument by using terms which we deem more adequate to
the proper interpretation. The concessions Rome makes in reference to
solemn profession and papal dispensation will certainly have to be considered exceptions to Romans 7:2, 3 if we proceed on the premise of the
kind of appeal she makes to the passage concerned.

[21] Cf. *Synopsis Theologiae Dogmaticae* as cited; Joseph Pohle: *op. cit.*,
pp. 184 ff. The latter says, "Every marriage between baptised persons,
whether consummated or not, is intrinsically indissoluble" (p. 184).

remains inviolate and applies to all other unconsummated marriages just as rigidly as it does to consummated marriages. It follows therefore that Rome regards Romans 7:2, 3 as applicable to unconsummated marriage. And so we are compelled to press the question again: where is the evidence to show that Paul could be properly regarded as envisaging or allowing the circumstance that marriage had not yet been consummated by the conjugal act as legitimating the suspension of the principle of Romans 7:2, 3 in the two exceptional cases alleged by Rome? And to press the question one step further, what warrant is there for supposing that Paul could have granted the propriety of certain exceptions in the case of unconsummated marriage and yet could not possibly be regarded as envisaging any exception to consummated marriage? Apologists for the Romish position must surely find it difficult to discover any Biblical evidence to substantiate their contention. That is to say, they must find it hard to find warrant for the sharp line of distinction drawn on this question between consummated and unconsummated marriage so long as they concede that Romans 7:2, 3 has relevance to unconsummated as well as to consummated marriage. The plain fact is that Romish theologians waive appeal to Scripture when they proceed to validate the exceptions claimed. They appeal rather to tradition and to the primacy of the Roman pontiff.[22] And once this is done it is apparent that appeal to Scripture is no longer necessary. It is equally apparent that the kind of evidence upon which we insist is not forthcoming and is really not available. In other words, the Scripture itself does not support the Romish position on the question now at issue and, as far as argument based on Scripture is concerned, the Romish appeal to Romans 7:2, 3 is patently inconsistent. This inconsistency should be obvious to any Protestant, for it is an inconsistency demonstrated by the very logic inherent in the necessity of appeal to tradition and to the primacy of the pontiff, a necessity fully acknowledged by Romanists themselves.

We must, however, carry the argument as it respects Rome's appeal to Romans 7:2, 3 one step further. This concerns I Corinthians 7:15. Rome claims the right of dissolution

---

[22] *Cf.* Joseph Pohle: *op. cit.*, pp. 201 ff.; Arthur Devine: *op. cit.*, pp. 90 f.

a vinculo in the instance of what is called the Pauline privilege.²³
In this case the right of dissolution applies even to consummated marriage, though not, of course, to consummated marriage between Christians. The Pauline privilege has reference
merely to what Rome calls marriage *legitimum* and *consummatum* but not *ratum*. It should be understood that our
argument in reference to the Romish position at this point is
not premised on any necessary disagreement with the Romish
interpretation of I Corinthians 7:15 other than to dissent
emphatically from the indefensible extensions given to the
Pauline privilege in Romish application. The arbitrary ampli-
fications²⁴ given to this privilege by Rome's official spokesmen
betrays the laxity of interpretation and of application which
Rome can conveniently avow and shows the practical nullity
thereby afforded to her vaunted strictness in the matter of
marital sanctity. But apart from the question of Romish
looseness in these regards, all that needs to be recognised at
present is that Rome sanctions the right of divorce in the case
of I Corinthians 7:15 and that we are not now concerned to
dispute the propriety of this interpretation *per se*.

The question is: how does this affect the interpretation of
Romans 7:2, 3 and, in particular, Rome's appeal to this passage in support of the indissolubility of the marriage bond?
It is not needless to mention that I Corinthians 7:15 is no less
Pauline than Romans 7:2, 3. Apart from the question of the
chronology of the composition of these two epistles (a matter
not without bearing upon the whole question of harmony),
the inspiration and authority of Paul's teaching, even on
Rome's own presuppositions, would require us to maintain
the complete harmony of the two passages. I Corinthians
7:15 is compatible with Romans 7:2, 3. But when Paul
penned Romans 7:2, 3 he made no allusion to I Corinthians
7:15; the terms of the former passage are quite absolute and
universal and, in themselves, suggest or express no exception.

²³ *Synopsis Theologiae Dogmaticae* as cited, pp. 155 ff.; Joseph Pohle:
op. cit., pp. 208 ff.; Arthur Devine: *op. cit.*, pp. 85 ff.; *A Commentary on
the New Testament* as cited, pp. 460 f.
    ²⁴ See Joseph Pohle: *op. cit.*, pp. 211 ff.; Arthur Devine: *op. cit.*, pp.
87 f.; *Synopsis Theologiae Dogmaticae*, pp. 157 ff.

How are we to explain this on the assumption that there is in reality the exception of I Corinthians 7:15?

At this point it is well to bear in mind what has been argued above respecting the universal obligation and application of Romans 7:2, 3. It will not do to say that here Paul has in view a principle that is applicable only to Christian marriage, to use Rome's terminology, marriage *ratum* as distinguished from marriage that is merely *legitimum*. Paul surely states a principle that applies to the institution of marriage as such and to restrict it to marriage between Christians would open the door to abuses that would run completely counter to the sanctity which the Scripture recognises as belonging to all valid and legitimate marriage, a sanctity which will have to be recognised as implicit in the teaching of Paul in the immediately preceding context of I Corinthians 7:15, namely verses 12–14, as well as in Romans 7:2, 3. It is quite true that in Romans 7:1 Paul has in mind the Mosaic law when he says to his readers, "For I speak to them that know the law", and he assumes on that basis that they should readily acknowledge the validity of the principle that the law has dominion over a man as long as he lives. Furthermore, when he adduces his example in verses 2 and 3 we shall have to suppose that the Mosaic law is distinctly in view. That is just saying that Paul has in view the special revelation of the Old Testament as that which should place beyond dispute for his readers the validity of the principle asserted in verse 1 and the specific example of the application of that principle alluded to in verses 2 and 3. But it by no means follows that it is only within the area of the *knowledge* of that Mosaic law that the general principle stated in verse 1 and the specific principle enunciated in verses 2 and 3 are operative or applicable. It is one thing to appeal to special revelation to show that a certain obligation rests upon men; it is another thing to hold that the obligation rests only upon those who possess that revelation. In this particular case there is no ground for believing that Paul regarded the principles set forth in Romans 7:1–3 as applicable only to those who were in the advantageous position of knowing the Mosaic law. Still further, if the principles applied only to believers we can readily detect what havoc this would entail for the doctrine that Paul proceeds to unfold in verse 4. His doctrine is, in effect, that all men are under the bondage of the law and are bound to that bondage until they become dead to the law by the body of Christ. How would it fare with this doctrine if the principle of the analogy by which he illustrates the doctrine were not as universal within its own specific sphere as the doctrine itself? Consequently we must conclude that the principle, to wit, that the married woman is bound by law to her husband as long as he lives, must apply to marriage as such and therefore to the very marriage contemplated by Paul in I Corinthians 7:12–14. And so the question confronts us in all its acuteness: how does the concession of I Corinthians 7:15, a concession which Rome acknowledges is warrant for the dissolution of the marriage bond, comport with Romans 7:2, 3?

If Rome is to answer this question on the basis of Scripture principles, she will have to admit that Paul recognises that there is at least one exception to the rule of Romans 7:2, 3, in other words, that there is one case where a woman may remarry prior to the death of her first husband and yet not be called an adulteress. It follows, therefore, on these premises, that when we assert the principle of Romans 7:2, 3 we have at the same time in mind this one exception and that Paul likewise had it in mind. Yet because it was an extraordinary and exceptional case and, within the orbit of its own peculiar exigencies taken for granted, it was not necessary for Paul to mention the exception and so could assert the principle in terms which are in themselves absolute. So Rome should have to admit that when Romans 7:2, 3 is cited to support the indissolubility of the bond of consummated marriage there is the tacit understanding that one exception holds good, namely, the case of I Corinthians 7:15.

At the present time we are not again entering upon the debate as to whether or not adultery is a proper ground for the dissolution of the marriage bond. That question has been debated earlier in this study. All that we wish to do now is simply to show the *non sequitur* of the type of appeal Rome makes to Romans 7:2, 3 in order to disprove the legitimacy of dissolution on that ground. Once it is allowed that there is any ground upon which the dissolution of consummated marriage may take place (and this Rome admits in the instance of the Pauline privilege), then Romans 7:2, 3 admits of an exception. And if it admits of one exception, why may it not also admit of another? If it admits of an exception there cannot be any offhand appeal to Romans 7:2, 3 in support of the indissolubility of the marriage bond as if its intent and import were as absolute and exclusive as its express terms appear to imply. But this is precisely the kind of use that Rome makes of the passage in the polemic for her own doctrine of indissolubility. This is what we must deem to be invalid and unfair. It is such for the simple reason that the citation of Romans 7:2, 3 in this way creates the impression that Rome, in contrast with those who claim dissolubility on the ground of adultery, stands for the terms of Romans 7:2, 3 without any equivocation or exception, when, as a matter of fact, she herself entertains an exception which is just as directly an exception to Romans 7:2, 3 as is the exception for the cause of adultery. Rome, no more than traditional Protestants, carries into operation the absolute and exceptionless terms of Romans 7:2, 3. And she may not cite it and quote it as if she did.

The question is, however, still before us: how are we to reconcile Romans 7:2, 3 with the position taken in this series of studies that adultery is a legitimate ground of divorce? Our position in reference to this question is not as easy as it might be if we took unequivocally the position of Rome regarding the Pauline privilege. For then we could use the argument pleaded above that there is at least one exception and, if so, there is no reason why there should not also be a second, provided the Scripture affords us sufficient evidence in favour of that conclusion. We have taken the position that while the preponderance of the evidence appears to support the view that Paul contemplates dissolution in the precise conditions envisaged in I Corinthians 7:15, yet we have not dogmatically affirmed this to be the only feasible interpretation. Hence dogmatic appeal to I Corinthians 7:15 as providing a clear case of exception to the rule of Romans 7:2, 3 cannot be made, and we are compelled to limit ourselves to the one exception, namely, adultery. We are keenly aware of the difficulty which such a position involves, and we appreciate anew the force that can be given to the question: do not the absolute terms of Romans 7:2, 3 require us to revise our conclusions respecting adultery as a valid ground of divorce and, in particular, revise our interpretation of Matthew 19:9?

To this question we are still compelled to give a negative answer. The reasons given earlier for interpreting Matthew 19:9 as legitimating divorce for adultery, we believe, are valid. And hence we are now required to show why Romans 7:2, 3 does not demand a revision of that judgment.

As argued above, Paul asserts in Romans 7:2, 3 a *basic* law respecting marriage, a law as universal in its obligation as is the general principle that the law has dominion over a man so long as he lives. This emphasis upon the *basic* character of this law may seem to offer the one insuperable objection to the supposition that adultery is a proper ground for divorce. However much this may appear to be the case we cannot and must not tone down the relentlessness of the law that a woman is bound by the law of her husband as long as he lives. It is, strange as it may seem, this very feature that provides, in our judgment, the key to the solution of our problem. It is our thesis that divorce for adultery does not interfere with the unmitigated obligation and unrelenting principle to which Paul gives expression in the passage concerned.

What Paul is stressing here is the binding law that governs marriage. There is, it must be emphasised, in reality no exception to that law, and that is just saying that there is no circumstance under which the woman may regard herself as free from that law and at liberty to violate it. The woman must *always* recognise that she is under the law of her husband and that deviation from conjugal fidelity will mean for her the sin and disgrace of adultery. This obligation to conjugal fidelity continues throughout the whole life of her husband and the very suggestion of exception to such a law would be an ethical abomination.

It should not be regarded, however, as incompatible with this emphasis upon binding and invariable law to conceive of the woman as being relieved from this law of her husband by some kind of action for which she has no responsibility but which involves a complete dereliction of fidelity and desecration of the sanctity of the marriage bond on the part of her husband. And we can surely recognise that if, in such an event, the woman were relieved from the law of her husband and from the obligation to conjugal fidelity, this release would not constitute a violation on her part of the principle and obligation which we have repeatedly asserted to be the unvarying law and rule of her conduct. For, in such a case, she would not have transgressed the law of her husband nor would she have done anything to release herself from that law: she would be wholly the victim of the desecration of a relationship to which she is party while in no sense party to the desecration itself. In other words, her relation to that unfaithful husband may well be conceived of as radically altered without any infringement on her part of the law that binds her, and so radically altered that she may regard herself as released from that law.

This is what we do find in the case of adultery. For, if adultery gives to the innocent spouse the right of divorce and remarriage, it means that the action on the part of the guilty spouse has so radically affected the relationship that release is thereby secured from the law that previously bound the innocent party. Thinking in terms of the woman as the innocent spouse this release is not properly conceived of, in the final analysis, as an exception to the law of her husband but as an abnormal and exceptional situation in view of which she may be released from the law of her husband.

The question will be asked: why did not Paul make allowance for this abnormal situation since it involves so notable an exception to the rule, "So then if while her husband lives she be married to another man she shall be called an adulteress"? The answer is that we can rather readily detect how extraneous it would be to the purpose Paul had in mind and how contrary it would be to the very principle he is asserting to take into account the wholly abnormal and extreme contingency of adultery. The fact is that the right of dissolution on the ground of adultery is not really an exception to the principle Paul is stating. The effect of divorce in the case of adultery is not to suspend the operation of the principle and of the obligation. The case is rather that adultery introduces a new set of conditions under which the principle and obligation concerned may be regarded as no longer applicable in respect of the innocent spouse.[25] In other words, the contingency of perverse and wanton violation of marital sanctity need not be taken into consideration when appeal is made to the law that governs marriage. For when stress is laid on the law that binds and upon the grievous wrong entailed in the violation of that law the thought is focused on the fulfilment of all the conditions and proprieties inherent in the marital relation and obligation. It would detract from this emphasis to suggest what provisions may obtain for the person concerned when a new complex of factors radically alters the conditions presupposed in the assertion of the obligation. To intimate the provisions for such an exceptional circumstance would defeat, or at any rate perplex, the precise emphasis of the apostle. This consideration should explain why there is no allusion in this text or context to the right of divorce and remarriage in the event of adultery on the part of the other spouse and should show how this passage is compatible with the view that divorce on that ground is legitimate. Although divorce for adultery does contemplate a situation in which the woman as the innocent party may marry another man and yet not be called an adulteress, it is very questionable if this may properly be spoken of as an exception to verse 3 as envisioned here by the apostle. The rule as stated by Paul has in view the fact that the woman is under obligation to undeviating marital fidelity. To this obligation there is no exception and the exceptionless character of the obligation is enforced by the fact that if she does violate such fidelity she shall be called an adulteress. The same principle applies, of course, *mutatis mutandis* to the husband.

It was said at an earlier stage of our discussion that in verses 2 and 3 Paul must still have in mind the provisions of the Mosaic law, because he alludes to the Mosaic law in verse 1. It is possible, therefore, that Paul has in mind very specifically the provisions of Deuteronomy 24:1–4. If so, then there is a

---

[25] It is precisely this situation that must be applied in the case of I Corinthians 7:15 if we are to regard that passage as legitimating dissolution of the bond of marriage. Otherwise such an interpretation of I Cor. 7:15 will have to be abandoned.

very ostensible reason why he should speak of the *woman* as being bound to the law of her husband rather than of the man as being bound to the law of his wife. According to the Deuteronomy passage a man was permitted to put away his wife, but no provision was in effect whereby a woman could put away her husband. Hence Paul could speak only of the wife as bound and not *vice versa*. If the interpretation and application of verses 2 and 3 are thus conceived of very strictly in terms of such Mosaic provisions, the relevance of this passage to the whole question of divorce in the New Testament is greatly decreased. For, in this event, Paul would simply be eliciting from the Old Testament a specific example, which was well-adapted to his purpose, to illustrate a specific application of the general principle of verse 1. He could use it to good advantage because it was familiar to his readers and provided him also with an analogy well-suited to the purpose of illustrating the doctrine of verse 4. The effect which such a view would have upon the question now in debate can be readily seen when we remember that, according to Deuteronomy 24:1–4, the woman, though not at liberty to divorce her husband and though bound to him for life as far as any action she could initiate was concerned, was nevertheless at liberty to marry another if divorced by her husband. On such remarriage she was not called, or regarded as, an adulteress. We can see, therefore, that Paul in verse 3 would not be taking into account any of the provisions that may obtain when the woman is subjected to a certain kind of action on the part of her husband. He does not take account of what the woman may properly do when another complex of factors enters into her situation. We can also see the reason why: it would detract from the real point of his illustration and thoroughly perplex the course of his argument. His illustration was perfectly good and universally valid within the conditions presupposed and envisaged. In like manner, the bearing of this passage upon our problem would be greatly simplified, for it would be perfectly apparent that Paul would not be reflecting upon the question as to what the woman may do in the event of adultery on the part of her husband any more than is he reflecting upon what the woman might do under the Mosaic law if she were divorced by her husband. We could plead the obvious omission of reference to some Mosaic provisions as proof that the text was not intended to prescribe a rule to be applied to all conditions and circumstances and, consequently, as not providing us with any light on the law of God as it applies in the case of adultery.

It must be remembered that this is a distinctly possible interpretation of Romans 7:2, 3. It should not be ruled out as unreasonable. This fact should be given due consideration as we view all angles of our question. For if, on the one hand, the legitimacy of divorce and remarriage on the ground of adultery is maintained and if, on the other, the type of treatment accorded to Romans 7:2, 3 in this chapter does not commend itself, then a reasonable resolution of the difficulty may be secured by adopting this interpretation.

The present writer is not ready, however, to adopt such a view of Romans 7:2, 3 and therefore not prepared to rest the solution upon such an interpretation. To say the least, it is possible that Paul, though having the Mosaic law very distinctly in mind, intends nevertheless to assert a principle that is universally valid and operative, and operative therefore even when the permissions of Deuteronomy 24:1–4 have been abrogated. Since this is so, we may not allow the provisions of Deuteronomy 24:1–4 to determine our interpretation and application of the principles enunciated. To make our interpretation dependent upon the assumption that certain provisions are regarded by Paul as in operation, when we may not be warranted in making this assumption, would be precarious.

It would also appear that there is a much more reasonable and cogent consideration why Paul should have referred to the woman in this case rather than to the man. It is the use which he is to make of the analogy. The doctrine he is illustrating is the death of the believer to the law by the body of Christ and the believer's union with Christ in the power of his resurrection. The main point of the similitude is that the woman is released from the law of her husband by his death and is therefore at liberty to be married to another. And the doctrine illustrated is that the believer is freed from the law by the death of Christ so that he may be married to another, the risen Christ. It is apparent that in the similitude it is only the woman who can appropriately represent the believer because in the union of the believer with Christ it is Christ who takes the place of the husband and therefore the woman must take the place of the believer.

Furthermore, there is the consideration arising from I Corinthians 7:39, which is practically identical with Romans 7:2. In the former passage we cannot suppose that any of the peculiar conditions or provisions of Deuteronomy 24:1–4 are in view: Paul is looking at the marital relation from the standpoint of the principles and provisions that are permanently operative and binding in the Christian economy. It is entirely more feasible to regard Romans 7:2, 3 as parallel in this respect to I Corinthians 7:39, and that both passages will have to be interpreted and applied in the same way in reference to the question of divorce. It may also be added that in seeking to harmonise I Corinthians 7:39 with the position that adultery is a legitimate ground of divorce the same treatment would have to be accorded this passage and the same line of argument applied as in the case of Romans 7:2, 3.

IV

Practical Cases

In bringing this series of studies to a close it is necessary to discuss certain questions, some of which have been alluded to in earlier chapters, and also to deal with some practical cases in order to illustrate the application of the principles derived from our study of the Scripture teaching.

A. *The Rights of the Woman.* On the basis of Matthew 5:32; 19:9 we have found that the man has the right to divorce his wife for the cause of adultery.[1] These two passages say nothing overtly regarding a similar right for the woman in the event of adultery on the part of her husband. Are we to suppose that this right of divorce is confined to the man? We have found that Mark 10:12 is particularly instructive in this regard.[2] As far as the Gospels are concerned this is the only passage in which there is allusion to divorce on the part of the woman — "and if she, having put away her husband, marry another, she commits adultery".

It is to be noted, of course, that here the right of divorce is not reflected upon. The force of the passage is prohibitory. In verse 11 what is prohibited is that a man should put away his wife and marry another. And the sin involved is that, if he does these two things, he commits adultery against his wife. Verse 12, by implication, applies the same prohibition to the woman and asserts that if a woman puts away her husband and marries another she, in like manner, does wrong. The sin specified in this case is that she commits adultery.

Nevertheless the significant feature is that Mark 10:12 does contemplate the possibility of divorce on the part of the woman and presupposes such an eventuality. The social order as envisaged is one in which divorce proceedings could be

[1] See pp. 20 f., 33 ff.
[2] See pp. 52 ff.

initiated by the woman. And though the kind of divorce in view is conceived of as morally wrong and therefore illegitimate, yet the way is opened for the inference that, if divorce for a proper reason were brought into the purview, it would be the right of the woman as well as of the man to initiate such a divorce process. And once we grant that the man has the right of divorce for adultery, Mark 10:12 provides strong presumption in favour of the conclusion that while the woman may not, any more than the man, divorce her spouse and marry another without the proper ground, yet, on the proper ground, she may, no less than the man, sue for divorce.

In I Corinthians 7:15 we have rather strong corroboration of this inference. There the man and the woman are placed on the same level as respects the liberty granted. "But if the unbelieving depart, let him depart: the brother or the sister is not bound in such cases." The preponderance of the considerations is in favour of regarding this liberty as that of dissolution of the marriage bond, at least freedom from the bond of marriage. If this is the correct interpretation, then to the believing woman as well as to the believing man is accorded the right to dissolve the bond of marriage or to regard the bond as dissolved in the event of desertion by an unbelieving partner. If this is so in the event of such desertion, it would surely follow that the same right would belong to the woman in the case of adultery on the part of her husband. This instance, then, would offer not simply the argument of presumption but that of conclusive inference required by analogy.

Even if we were to regard I Corinthians 7:15 as granting simply freedom from bed and board, freedom from the necessity of cohabitation, there would still be an indication of the equality between man and woman in reference to this marital question. It would still mark out the direction in which New Testament thought points, namely, the obliteration of the distinction between man and woman in respect of the matter with which we are now dealing.

It is here, however, that a general principle of New Testament teaching needs to be appreciated and applied. Obviously the New Testament does not obliterate the distinction between the sexes. The ineradicable distinction established in creation and exemplified in divine ordinance is fully recognised and is applied in a great many concrete situations. Yet in several respects, in contradistinction from the Old Testament, there is no longer male nor female, as there is no longer Jew nor Gentile. And surely it is necessary to believe that in respect of this basic question of marital relationship the same rights and liberties are granted to the woman as are granted to the man when her spouse violates conjugal fidelity. And so the indication given in Mark 10:12 and the clear equality expressed in I Corinthians 7:15 are to be interpreted in the light of this more general principle. These passages verify the legitimacy of applying the general principle to this specific situation.

B. *The Right of Remarriage.* We have taken the position, on what we believe to be proper grounds, that the man who puts away his wife for adultery may remarry without committing an offence; the exceptive clause in Matthew 19:9 applies to the remarriage as well as to the putting away.[3] If this is so, then the same privilege would belong to the woman who puts away her husband for adultery. This would be a necessary extension of the foregoing conclusion. The question that arises here, however, is the status of the guilty spouse in the case of divorce for adultery. The innocent spouse is free to marry again. What about the guilty spouse? Is he or she free to remarry? Exegetically this is largely the question of the interpretation of Matthew 5:32b; Luke 16:18b (*cf.* Matthew 19:9b). The text of Matthew 19:9b is a matter of debate. For our present interest it is not necessary to try to settle the question of the proper text. There is no question regarding the genuineness of the text in Matthew 5:32b and Luke 16:18b. Consequently even should we conclude that Matthew 19:9b does not belong to Matthew's text here, there need be no question regarding the authenticity of the saying. The text of Matthew 5:32b and Luke 16:18b have the same meaning and effect. So in whatever form we take it, whether in the form of Matthew 5:32b — "and whoever marries her who has been put away (a divorced woman) commits adultery", or in the form of Luke 16:18b — "and he who marries

---

3 See pp. 33 ff.

her who has been put away from her husband commits adultery", the question is posed for us: does this apply to every divorced woman and, by implication *mutatis mutandis*, to every divorced man, whether divorced with or without the legitimate reason? There can be no question but it applies to the person divorced without the proper ground. The reason for this is that when spouses are divorced without proper cause they are still man and wife in the sight of God. Consequently, other conjugal relations by either is adultery just as surely as if the divorce had never taken place. But the question is greatly perplexed when we consider the case of legitimate divorce. What about the guilty divorcee in such an event?

This question cannot be dismissed lightly. For it is not obvious, either in Matthew 5:32b or in Luke 16:18b or in Matthew 19:9b (supposing that here the clauses in question are genuine), that more is meant than the illegitimate divorce which is patently the burden of all three passages. It must be borne in mind that the main thrust of all the passages is not the legitimacy of divorce for adultery but the illegitimacy of divorce for any other reason. To such an extent is this the case in Luke 16:18 that no exception is mentioned. We infer that allowance is made for the exception only by the analogy of Matthew 5:32; 19:9. And even in the two latter passages, where the exception is expressly mentioned, it is also apparent that it is not the exception that is in the foreground but rather that there is no other exception. Consequently it may well be that it is the main thrust of these passages that is in view in Matthew 5:32b and Luke 16:18b, that is to say, the divorced woman contemplated in what is the main burden of both verses and not the woman contemplated in the exception. If this inference is correct then the woman divorced for adultery would not be in view when it is said, "whoever marries her who has been put away commits adultery" (Matt. 5:32b).

There are, however, more specific considerations which favour this conclusion. In Matthew 5:32a the exact terms have to be noted again. They are: "every one who puts away his wife except for the cause of fornication makes her to suffer adultery". Now when we ask the question, what woman is made to suffer adultery? the answer is, undoubtedly the woman who is put away without the adequate cause. It is not the woman who is put away for the cause of fornication, for the latter is not made "to suffer adultery"; she committed adultery prior to her being put away. Hence, when we pass on to the latter part of the verse and read, "whoever marries her who has been put away commits adultery", we should reasonably infer that the divorced woman in mind is the woman who has been made to suffer adultery and not the woman who had previously committed adultery and for that reason had been legitimately divorced by her husband.

We can at least say that we are not warranted in stating definitely and conclusively that the woman divorced for adultery is included in the two clauses in question in Matthew 5:32b and Luke 16:18b. We are left therefore with the possibility that the woman who has been divorced for adultery is not to be regarded as committing another act of adultery when, after being divorced, she contracts another marriage, and that the man who marries her is not to be regarded as thereby committing adultery. What constrains this conclusion is strictly the exegetical considerations governing the relevant passages. We may not impose upon these passages a meaning which they do not clearly bear.

There is also another consideration that bears upon this question. In the event of divorce for adultery the marriage has been dissolved. It is for that reason that the innocent spouse may remarry. But if the marriage has been dissolved, it is difficult to see on what ground the contracting of another marriage on the part of the guilty divorcee could be considered adultery. What constituted the prior act of infidelity an act of adultery was the fact that the marriage was still inviolate. But once the marriage has been dissolved there is a very different relationship. And we must remember that in the case of divorce for adultery it is by divine warrant that the marriage is dissolved. The parties are no longer man and wife. If so, it is difficult to discover any biblical ground on the basis of which to conclude that the remarriage of the guilty divorcee is to be considered in itself an act of adultery and as constituting an adulterous relation.

It can be argued, of course, on the other side of the question that, if the legitimacy of remarriage on the part of the guilty party to a divorce for adultery is conceded, this opens the door to gross license. For example, the man who wants another woman rather than his wife may resort to the expedient of committing adultery in order to be released from the existing marital bond and, on being divorced, marry the other woman who has stolen his affection or whose affection he has stolen. This would seem to place a premium upon adultery as the convenient means of securing the dissolution of one marriage and of contracting another. Whereas, if the position were taken that the remarriage of the guilty party to a divorce for adultery is illegitimate and adulterous, this would serve as one of the most effective deterrents of license and would bring one of the strongest inducements to fidelity to bear upon those tempted to conjugal unfaithfulness.

It must be admitted that very grave abuses follow upon the position that the remarriage of the guilty divorcee is not *per se* adultery. Any one who is sensitive to the requirements of purity and is jealous for the interests of chastity is alive to the danger of these abuses. But the mere fact that grave abuse is only too liable to enter does not disprove the position itself. How great is the abuse that attends divorce for adultery! How many there are who resort to this means of securing divorce! But the abuse does not annul the fact that it is by divine warrant that such divorce is legitimated. The legitimation of divorce for such a reason does not minimise the sin of adultery; it rather stresses the gravity of the desecration that adultery entails. And divorce is not intended to give any license in the matter of adultery. The Scripture recognises the abuse to which the legitimacy of divorce for adultery is liable to be subjected. Yet it does not for that reason forbid such divorce.

In reference to the question at issue the case is simply that we are not able to find biblical warrant for affirming that the person who has been divorced for adultery commits another act of adultery when he or she remarries. It should be remembered, of course, that adultery is a crime punishable by the civil magistrate and censurable by the church. The church must unsparingly condemn all adultery as also all other forms of sexual uncleanness. In the discipline of its members the church must be vigilant and faithful. All known adultery must be disciplined with the appropriate censures. The person who has been divorced for adultery necessarily comes under grave censure, such censure as would necessarily involve suspension from privileges until such time as evidence is given of adequate repentance. In the case of a person who has remarried after such divorce the gravity of the offence for which divorce was secured must not be minimised. The anomaly of the second marriage and the shame attaching to the sin that made it possible are to be fully appreciated and stressed. The discipline of the church must take such sin and anomaly into its purview in order that the honour of Christ and the purity of the church may be preserved. But the church in the exercise of discipline must not go beyond the warrant of Scripture. And to categorise the second marriage in such a case as an act of adultery and to discipline accordingly do not appear to rest upon the requisite evidence.

It does not necessarily follow, however, that we have sufficient evidence on the basis of which we may pronounce this second marriage legitimate. It is one thing to say that we do not have warrant for declaring it illegitimate. It is another thing to pronounce it to be legitimate. In the case of the innocent party to divorce the exceptive clause in Matthew 19:9 gives us warrant to declare his or her remarriage to be legitimate. But we do not have such warrant in the case of the guilty party. Hence the situation in which we are placed is that, while, on the one hand, we may not declare the remarriage of the guilty party to be illegitimate and adulterous yet, on the other hand, we may not declare it to be legitimate. That appears to be the position in which the relevant evidence leaves us. This does not mean that the second marriage is neither right nor wrong. It simply means that we are not in a position to declare dogmatically one way or the other. We must be humble enough to recognise the limitations of our knowledge, a fact with which we have to reckon sometimes in very practical matters.

In reference to the teaching and discipline of the church this position would amount to this. The person divorced for adultery who remarries after divorce may not be regarded as having committed adultery thereby nor as living in an adulterous relation. The church may not discipline the act as such nor the resulting relation; it may not require the parties to separate from one another. But the church may not teach that this kind of remarriage is legitimate, and it may not place upon such remarriage its imprimatur and benediction.

C. *Separation without Dissolution.* The Romish Church teaches that there may be separation from bed and board without dissolution of the bond of marriage. It is this limited kind of divorce (*divortium a toro et mensa*) that the Church of Rome allows in the event of adultery. This introduces us to a subject reflected on earlier but which was not discussed at length. The real question is whether spouses may *properly* separate from one another and terminate the discharge of conjugal debts without severing the bond of marriage. It might appear that I Corinthians 7:11 provides us with an example of this kind of separation by which the spouses may mutually agree to separate from one another or by which one spouse may properly leave the other or by which one spouse may properly expel the other. It is necessary to controvert this interpretation of I Corinthians 7:11. It is true that I Corinthians 7:11 envisages *de facto* separation. But it has been shown that the separation in view is not contemplated as legitimate.[4] Suffice it to recall the context. "But to the married I give charge, not I but the Lord, that the wife depart not from her husband . . . and that the husband leave not his wife" (vss. 10, 11). The parenthetical statement in verse 11 — "but and if she depart, let her remain unmarried or be reconciled to her husband" — simply provides that if, contrary to this commandment, separation actually takes place another marriage must not be contracted. To suppose that the parenthetical statement enunciates what might be called a provision of separation is to load the statement concerned beyond all warrant.[5] The parenthesis does not *sanction* separation; it

4 See pp. 61 ff.
5 Calvin's comments on this passage are sober and to the point. "But as to his commanding the wife, who is separated from her husband, to *remain unmarried*, he does not mean by this that separation is allowable, nor does he give permission to the wife to live apart from her husband; but if she has been expelled from the house, or has been put away, she must not think that even in that case she is set free from his power; for it is not in the power of a husband to dissolve marriage. He does not

simply recognises that it may take place. Hence we conclude
that the Word of God, neither in this passage nor elsewhere,
provides for and sanctions separation apart from dissolution
of the marriage bond. Divorce for adultery is by divine sanction; it is a divinely instituted provision for a certain situation
and it dissolves the bond of marriage. But there is no such
divine provision for mere separation. The divine institution
is that those united in the bond of marriage are bound to the
mutual discharge of all marital debts until the bond is severed
by death or by dissolution on a proper ground.

In taking this position it is necessary to guard against mis-
understanding. It is fully acknowledged that spouses, for
various reasons and for longer or shorter periods, may not be
able to cohabit. On occasion this may be true for the greater
part of life. One partner may be the victim of disease, physical
or mental, by reason of which the spouses are not able to live
together. Normal marital relations may be thereby inter-
rupted and the discharge of certain conjugal debts may not
be possible any longer. Sometimes partners may be forcibly
separated from one another, as in the case of war and the
various tragedies and dislocations attendant upon it. Neither
partner may have any individual fault in connection with

therefore give permission here to wives to withdraw, of their own accord,
from their husbands, or to live away from their husband's establishment,
as if they were in a state of widowhood; but declares, that even those who
are not received by their husbands, continue to be bound, so that they
cannot take other husbands.

"But what if a wife is wanton, or otherwise incontinent? Would it not be
inhuman to refuse her the remedy, when constantly burning with desire?
I answer, that when we are prompted by the infirmity of our flesh, we must
have recourse to the remedy; after which it is the Lord's part to bridle and
restrain our affections by his Spirit, though matters should not succeed
according to our desire. For if a wife should fall into a protracted illness,
the husband would, nevertheless, not be justified in going to seek another
wife. In like manner, if a husband should, after marriage, begin to labour
under some distemper, it would not be allowable for his wife to change her
condition of life. The sum is this — God having prescribed lawful marriage
as a remedy for our incontinency, let us make use of it, that we may not,
by tempting him, pay the penalty of our rashness. Having discharged
this duty, let us hope that he will give us aid should matters go contrary
to our expectations" (*Commentary on the Epistles of Paul the Apostle to
the Corinthians*, English Translation, Edinburgh, 1848, Vol. I, pp. 239 f.).

such separations; they are involuntary and may be entirely contrary to the wishes of both. Furthermore, a faithful partner may be the victim of wantonness[6] on the part of the other. One spouse may have committed crime that involves imprisonment for a longer or shorter period, and forced separation is the result. Or, again, a faithful partner may be the victim of wilful desertion on the part of the other and may be required to bear patiently this *de facto* separation. In these latter two cases it is not wrong for the faithful and innocent spouse to be in the position of separation; for him or her it is a separation that is involuntary and forced by the criminality or wilfulness of the other. In either case the sin on the part of the faithless spouse is responsible for the separation that results, and for both the sin and the result the faithless spouse is to be condemned. There are also various other circumstances under which one or both spouses may be forced to endure *de facto* separation. The position now being propounded does not fail to recognise the complex factors which disturb the normalcy of marital life in numerous cases and makes full allowance for the separations which one or both partners may be innocently forced to endure. The whole point of the present thesis is simply that a spouse may not voluntarily separate himself or herself from the other spouse and thus wilfully refuse to perform the debts incident to the marital relation. And neither may the spouses by mutual consent agree thus to separate from one another. The Word of God makes no provision for such recourse or for such expedient. "What God hath joined together let not man put asunder." In other words, there is no warrant for supposing that God has instituted the provision of separation from bed and board to which recourse may properly be taken in cases where the dissolution of the marriage bond is not allowable. We must reckon with the fact that unless the marriage bond has been dissolved for a legitimate cause, the spouses are under obligation to live together in the discharge of all mutual debts unless, for some reason of divine providence beyond their control, they are compelled to be separated from one another. And they need to exercise great care that they do not misinterpret and misapply the provi-

[6] The words "wantonness" and "wanton" do not necessarily refer to unchaste behaviour.

dence of God so as to find in it an excuse by which to exculpate themselves of the tendency to relax full marital devotion.

It is necessary to stress this thesis because escape from the obligations and hardships of the married state by the despicable expedient of separation is so widespread. It is one of the ways in which the sanctity of the marriage bond is being desecrated, and even professing Christian people think that by separation without dissolution they can conserve the interests of the Christian ethic, maintain their good standing in the church, and, at the same time, relieve themselves of many embarrassments and encumbrances. The church, also, in dealing with concrete situations is only too liable to resort to this expedient of separation as the advice to be given or as the requirement imposed upon certain couples whose marital relationship constitutes an embarrassing predicament for the church in the discharge of discipline. Separation without dissolution is no solution. If the marriage bond may not in the esteem of the church be dissolved for a scriptural reason or declared null and void by reason of its being invalid,[7] then the bond of marriage must be recognised as existing. And where it is recognised as existing it is the duty of the church to enjoin upon those thus united the discharge of their marriage vows and marital duties. The church must frankly face the consequences of the principles at stake and not condone or adopt the subterfuge of separation.

D. *Ecclesiastical Divorce.* Divorce in our modern situation is generally a matter that falls within the jurisdiction of the civil magistrate. It is not to be thought that this is an improper function of the state. Marriage deeply concerns the welfare of the community and it is within the province of the civil magistrate to regulate marriage and its dissolution. It is the right and duty of the state to prohibit certain marriages,

---

[7] Although the question of annulment has not been discussed in these studies, it is taken for granted that certain marriages are necessarily to be regarded as null and void, as, for example, marriages within the degrees of consanguinity and affinity forbidden by the Word of God. Such marriages are incestuous and should be annulled. Annulment differs from divorce. Divorce dissolves a marriage that legitimately exists. Annulment is a decree declaring the marriage to be null and void and therefore that in reality it did not exist.

PRACTICAL CASES   107

to grant divorce where such is proper, and to penalise infractions of those regulations which the state may properly impose.

It is apparent, however, that too frequently the laws of the state governing marriage and divorce are not in accord with the requirements of Scripture. Particularly is it the case that legislation respecting divorce is frequently too lax. And where the divorce laws diverge from Scripture they cannot be recognised by the church as valid and regulative for its procedure and discipline. It is here that a grave problem is posed for the Church that seeks to be faithful to the Word of God. To be specific, the church cannot recognise as proper many of the divorce decrees that are granted by the state and therefore cannot grant the legitimacy of the remarriage of parties who have been divorced on an unscriptural ground. Hence the endless perplexities that emerge and the painful ordeals through which ecclesiastical courts have to pass in order to decide faithfully and fairly on specific cases. In many instances it is not necessary or even feasible for the church to give any decree of divorce. In most cases all that the church is called upon to determine is whether or not a divorce granted by the state is proper and decide the issue of discipline, as it may arise, accordingly. But on occasion there does arise a case in which the interests of justice and equity require an ecclesiastical decree of divorce. Two examples will illustrate the necessity and *modus operandi* of such procedure.[8]

(1) A couple have been divorced by the state on an unscriptural ground. The woman, let us say, has been the victim of the wantonness of her husband. He wishes to be free from his marital obligations and secures a divorce, contrary to the woman's wishes and pleas, on an unscriptural ground. The woman, we are supposing, is quite innocent and is simply the victim of her husband's irresponsibility and faithlessness. This divorce the church cannot recognise as valid and, conse-

---

[8] It does not appear that this is an invasion on the part of the church of the prerogatives belonging to the state. In other words, it does not involve confusion of spheres. The prerogative exercised by the church in such cases is simply an application of the necessity of discipline. Discipline in certain cases requires the vindication of the guiltless as well as the censure or condemnation of the guilty.

quently, cannot consent to the remarriage of this innocent woman however sympathetic and regretful the church may and should be in the situation in which the woman finds herself.

But let us suppose that the wanton husband, under the protection of the divorce granted by the state, marries another woman. Thereby he has committed adultery. It is not reckoned as such by the state, but in reality that is what he has done. Because of this adultery the first wife now possesses a legitimate ground for divorce. She has a right (if not in this case, an obligation) to secure such divorce and thereafter she has the right to remarry. However, such divorce the state will not grant. It recognises the validity of the previous divorce and it would be retracting its own action and virtually acknowledging its own legalising of bigamy to grant another decree of divorce to this innocent woman. So the woman in question cannot now secure a divorce from her former husband on the proper and scriptural ground provided by her husband's act of adultery. What is to be done?

In many such cases, supposedly, the church proceeds on the assumption that the second marriage on the part of the man has given *ipso facto* the right to this divorced woman to remarry and recognises her remarriage as proper and valid. But this appears to be an unsatisfactory way of dealing with the question; it is not in the best interests of preserving the honour of Christ and of guarding the good name of the woman concerned. It is here that an ecclesiastical decree of divorce may and should operate.[9] The church, on the basis of the proper evidence of adultery on the part of this woman's husband — evidence in this case supplied by his second marriage —, should grant to this woman its own divorce decree. This would be a divorce on the proper ground and, being official, would have the effect of dissolving the marriage bond. This decree would also, by implication, declare the right of this woman to remarry. Whether she remarries or not, the ecclesi-

[9] If this action on the part of the church were regarded as simply an official declaration to the effect that the remarriage of the other spouse dissolved the former marriage rather than as an ecclesiastical decree of divorce, it makes no substantial difference to the argument involved and all the interests at stake would be conserved.

astical decree guards her honour and purity. If such procedure were practised by the church there is another wholesome by-product that would result. In many instances it would serve to inhibit the wanton unfaithfulness and haste so prevalent in our modern society. While it is true that many are so callous that an ecclesiastical decree would have no deterrent force, yet in the case of many others they would be constrained to behave themselves with more caution and restraint if they knew that on their remarriage after an unscriptural divorce the innocent victim of such divorce could secure a decree from an ecclesiastical court which would brand the unfaithful spouse as an adulterer. It would also vindicate the church's prerogative and guard the paths of justice. The restraining and ethicising influence might be very far-reaching.

(2) The other example concerns the state or commonwealth in which there is defective legislative or executive provision for the securing of divorce on a legitimate ground. It is conceivable that a state does not recognise the legitimacy of divorce for adultery.[10] A state governed by Roman Catholic dogma would be in this category. Or, even supposing that there is legislative provision for such divorce, it may be that the legal requirements are of such an involved and expensive character that many innocent people are not able to avail themselves of these facilities. Or it might be that the guilty partner or his accomplice or the proper witnesses to his or her guilt are not willing to make the proper acknowledgements before a civil court, while they are willing to do so before an ecclesiastical court. We can readily envisage a variety of situations in which an innocent partner to a marriage may be quite unable to secure a legitimate divorce from the civil authorities within whose jurisdiction he or she has domicile. In such circumstances ecclesiastical courts ought to exercise this prerogative on behalf of members who come within their jurisdiction and thus be able to give to innocent and deserving people the relief to which they are entitled according to the Word of God. In the case of adultery, proven by the requisite evidence before an ecclesiastical court, that court may issue

[10] This happens to be the case in the state of South Carolina. It does not permit divorce for any reason. We are not suggesting that South Carolina has taken its cue from Romish dogma.

the decree of dissolution so that the innocent spouse may be able to separate himself or herself from the offending partner. After such a decree is given, the innocent spouse justifiably separates from the guilty, and such separation carries with it nothing of the fault that attaches to separation without dissolution.

Complications may arise in such instances if the innocent partner wishes to remarry. If the state does not recognise the validity of the ecclesiastical decree then the state might regard the remarriage of this person as bigamous and penalise accordingly. But even granting that the person concerned will not be able to remarry because of the discrepancy between the law of the state and the law that governs the church, it does not at all follow that the church has not performed a necessary service in relieving the innocent person from a bond the sanctity of which has been desecrated and broken by the adultery of the faithless partner. We can readily see that there are situations in which the interests of purity and honour can be preserved only by the exercise of such an ecclesiastical prerogative.

E. *Cases.* In attempting to deal with particular cases it must be understood that it would be utterly impossible to discuss all eventualities. There is almost endless variety here and it is beyond the capacity of even the most competent analyst to review all actual, far less all possible, cases. At best we can only select a few instances in order to illustrate the application of biblical principles. Furthermore, we must bear in mind that certain cases are so complicated and entangled that they baffle conclusive solution. Any one who has encountered a fair sample of practical instances knows how exceedingly delicate and difficult some of these are. Sobriety demands that we be aware of our limitations and proceed with humility.

A great many of the problems that arise for us spring from the fact that the laws of the state do not conform to the law of Scripture. If, for example, divorce were granted only for scripturally legitimate reasons; a great many of these practical problems would disappear. The reason is simple. Illegitimate remarriage would largely disappear because the state would not permit remarriage except where there is legitimate divorce. If remarriage were contracted without legitimate divorce it would be penalised by the state as bigamy. State laws thoroughly conformed to Scripture would not eliminate all problems for the church. But they would greatly reduce the number of such. We are not, however, in any such ideal situation and consequently we have to reckon with the fact of numberless illegitimate divorces and remarriages. We might well despair if we did not believe, "Greater is he that is in you than he that is in the world".

Before proceeding to discuss particular cases there is one further matter that needs to be mentioned. A great deal of respect should be entertained for the position that when a person remarries after divorce on an unscriptural ground this remarriage should be regarded as invalid, that is to say, as null and void, and that the person concerned should be required to return to the former spouse. If this position were adopted it would make a great difference in the treatment of particular cases. In the discipline of the church the person concerned would be required to separate from the second spouse and return to the first. The condition of membership would be, at least, separation from the second and *readiness* to return to the first. We are inclined, however, to a different construction of the relationship constituted by the second marriage in such a case. The second marriage is undoubtedly adulterous and, therefore, illegitimate. But we are not prepared to say that it is invalid. For that reason our interpretation is that, though illegitimate, it is a real marriage and should be regarded as such. It has the effect of dissolving the first marriage, though, as we have seen above, there ought to be some kind of official action declaring or registering this virtual dissolution. On this interpretation the second marriage should not be dissolved. Though contracted and consummated illegitimately and adulterously, it nevertheless *de facto* exists and the parties to it should prove faithful to each other. It is admittedly a most anomalous situation. But it appears to be the most tenable view to recognise that marriages which are *de jure* illegitimate are still *de facto* existent, and since they are *de facto* existent they are thenceforth to be regarded as *de jure* binding. The parties have illegitimately pledged troth to one another and consummated that pledge in the conjugal act. That troth was wrong but it still binds them to observance of what was contracted and consummated by it. But let us now proceed to deal with specific cases.

(1) When divorce has been granted on an illegitimate ground and neither party remarries or indulges in illicit sexual relations they may and should come together again. That is to say, they ought to resume marital relations. This will require, of course, a cancellation or annulment of the decree of divorce. In reality they do not need to be remarried because the marriage had never really been dissolved. What procedure the state may require in order that the divorce may be annulled will no doubt differ in different states.

(2) When divorce has been given on a scriptural ground and neither party remarries there does not appear to be any reason why the divorced persons may not come together again on the repentance of the guilty party. In this case, however, the marriage would have to be contracted and consummated anew, for the simple reason that the former marriage had been dissolved.

(3) A divorce has been granted on an improper ground. The husband who sued for divorce remarries and thereby commits adultery. After some time his second wife dies. He repents of his wrong and wishes to return to his first spouse, who has in the interval remained unmarried. May he do so? And is remarriage necessary in such an event? There does not appear to be any good reason why the persons concerned may not resume marital relations. But it would appear to be necessary to contract and consummate a new marriage. The reason for this judgment is that although their marriage had not been dissolved by the divorce, yet the second marriage on the part of the husband, being adulterous, would have the effect of dissolving the first marriage. Even though the woman might not have secured a decree of dissolution on this ground, yet the total situation would be to the same effect.

(4) A husband has secured a divorce on an improper ground and remarries. After some time he divorces his second wife on an improper ground and wishes to return to his first wife. May he legitimately do so? The answer would appear to be

negative for the following reasons. The first marriage had not in reality, according to Scripture, been dissolved. The second marriage was therefore adulterous and, in accordance with what we have found in the preceding case, had the effect of dissolving the first marriage. The second marriage is the only one that exists. It cannot be dissolved by divorce on an improper ground. For this man to remarry his first wife would be another act of adultery with the added aggravation that the first wife also would now be involved in an adulterous union. We must recognise that the second marriage of this man though *de jure* illegitimate is nevertheless to be recognised as *de facto* existing and cannot be dissolved by divorce without proper cause. It is for this reason that he may not, in the situation posited, remarry his first wife.

(5) A woman has been divorced from her husband for the cause of adultery and she remarries. After a while her second husband dies. She is penitent for her sins and wishes to return to her first husband who has remained unmarried. May she do so? There are some who would apply Deuteronomy 24:4 to this case and infer that she would not be able to return to her first husband on the ground mentioned in this passage. This does not appear to be valid reasoning. It is apparent that the permission of Deuteronomy 24:1–3 was abrogated by our Lord. The Old Testament did not provide for divorce for adultery. It *permitted* divorce for other reasons. That permission our Lord in the exercise of his authority revoked and established the legitimacy of divorce for adultery. Since the permission of Deuteronomy 24:1–3 has been abrogated, it would hardly be feasible to regard the prohibition of Deuteronomy 24:4 as still applicable under the New Testament. Could the prohibition be regarded as still in force when the permission on which it rests has been abrogated? Hence the conclusion to which we are constrained to come is that Deuteronomy 24:4 could not be regarded as applying to this case. It would appear to be stretching the temporary regulations of the Old Testament beyond warrant to infer that Deuteronomy 24:4 would apply to New Testament divorce when the latter is of a very different character from that permitted in the Old Testament. Consequently we should

judge that the woman in question is not prohibited from being remarried to her first husband provided all other necessary safeguards are observed.

(6) Mr. and Mrs. A. have been divorced on an illegitimate ground, and Mr. and Mrs. B. likewise. Mr. A. marries Mrs. B. and Mr. B. marries Mrs. A. After a while, let us suppose, all four have become truly penitent and deplore their sin. They wish to put everything right. May they all resume their first marital relationships and thus return to their original partners? It is the judgment of the present writer that they may not. The reasons have really been given already. While it is not necessary to deal with all the possibilities of guilt and innocence in this quadrangular case, it must at least be said that the first remarriage, at least, was adulterous and had the effect of dissolving both marriages. The second pair of marriages are to be regarded as the only ones that are *de facto* existent. It would only aggravate the guilt of all concerned to try to remedy the situation by the method proposed. Truly penitent sinners will receive divine forgiveness and should be dealt with accordingly by the church of God. But they have often to bear all their life the shameful consequences of past transgression. It is for such persons to make that burden which they will have to bear the means of self-humiliation and sanctification.

(7) Mr. C. is guilty of adultery and Mrs. C. knows this. However, Mr. C. will not publicly confess to his sin and Mrs. C. cannot secure the necessary evidence to prove it before an ecclesiastical or civil court and thus cannot sue for a divorce on this proper ground. But Mr. C. is quite willing to be divorced on other grounds. May Mrs. C. secure a divorce on these improper grounds, knowing, of course, that the real ground is the adultery of which her husband is guilty but which she cannot prove? This is clearly a very difficult case. If we are to adhere to scriptural principles, however, we cannot give an affirmative answer. Divorce must be secured on the proper grounds. And if this woman is not able to plead such grounds before the court which is to grant the divorce, then she will have to endure her painful situation until such time as God in his providence will provide her with the evidence on the basis of which she may secure divorce for the proper

reason. Cases which elicit our deepest sympathy and sorrow often confront us. But we are compelled to recognise that innocent partners in marriage are often called upon to endure for longer or shorter periods a most distressing affliction from which they cannot escape without violating a divine institution and commandment. They do well patiently to bear their painful lot and to make the affliction the occasion for deeper reliance upon the grace of God.

(8) Mr. D. divorces Mrs. D. without adequate cause. Mrs. D. remarries and in doing so, of course, has committed adultery. May Mr. D. now remarry? If the question were, may Mrs. D. remarry on the remarriage of Mr. D. the answer would be very simple. On the remarriage of Mr. D., Mrs. D. could secure divorce on a proper ground and then remarry without fault. But the question here is perplexed by the fact that Mr. D. is implicated in the wrong of having divorced Mrs. D. without proper cause. And although Mrs. D. did commit an act of adultery by remarrying, yet that wrong on her part does not exculpate Mr. D. from the wrong of having put her away. Mr. D. is in the category of Matthew 5:32 — he made Mrs. D. to suffer adultery. May not this fact, that he is the guilty party in an illegitimate divorce, place him in an entirely different category respecting his right to remarry in the event of remarriage on the part of his divorced wife? It seems to the present writer that the Scripture does not provide us with the answer to this question. If our earlier arguments are correct then it would have to be granted that the remarriage of his divorced wife has the effect of dissolving the first marriage. That would appear to imply that Mr. D. is at liberty to remarry. But we may be prevented from drawing such a conclusion in this case because there rests upon Mr. D. the guilt of having made his wife to suffer adultery. Although the remarriage of Mrs. D. is adulterous, yet Mr. D. is implicated in that wrong, and it may be that this wrong deprives him of the right to remarry, a right which undoubtedly belongs to the innocent party to an improper divorce when the guilty party remarries. This case, therefore, seems to be in the same category as that of the right of remarriage on the part of the guilty party to a legitimate divorce. We are not able to answer dogmatically one way or the other.

(9) Mr. E. falls in love with another woman. Mrs. E. knows that she has lost her husband's matrimonial affection and devotion and that such have been transferred to the other woman. May she sue for a divorce on the ground that this is virtual adultery on the part of her husband, even though she has no reason for thinking that there has been any overt act of adultery? The answer to this question would be decisively in the negative. We have no ground for thinking that the Scripture warrants divorce in such a case for anything less than actual adultery.

Let us suppose that Mrs. E. secures a divorce on an improper ground, as, for example, incompatibility, and is thus separated from her husband. Obviously neither party is at liberty to remarry. If Mr. E. remarries, then our problem regarding the legitimacy of the remarriage of Mrs. E. is much the same as it is in the preceding case. If Mrs. E. remarries, *technically* Mr. E. would have the right to secure a divorce on the ground of Mrs. E's adulterous remarriage. But *morally*, in view of the misconduct on his part which precipitated the estrangement, his remarriage would be one loaded with reprehensible odium.

(10) Mr. and Mrs. F. have lived happily together for several years and have had children. After some time Mr. F. has become enamoured of another woman and desires to marry her. The state in which he lives grants divorce only for the cause of adultery. He publicly avows having committed adultery with this other woman and secures witnesses to testify before the court to adultery on his part. Divorce from Mrs. F. was granted. Thereupon Mr. F. married the other woman. He soon discovered his mistake but realised that he had made his bed and must bear the consequences. After some years, however, his second wife wished to be separated from him and he was able to secure a decree of nullity on the ground of her impotence. So the state decreed Mr. F's second marriage to be null and void. Mr. F. is penitent for his waywardness and wishes to return to his former wife and perform the duties of husband and father which he had renounced. He also alleges that the charge of adultery which he himself had instituted and on the basis of which the divorce had been granted was false and had simply been an expedient to meet the requirements of

the law. Mr. F's former wife, who had not remarried in the interval, is willing to have Mr. F. as her husband. May Mr. and Mrs. F. be remarried and resume marital relations? The answer to this question will have to be negative.

Even if we suppose that Mr. F's story is true and that no adultery had been committed prior to the divorce, yet the remarriage of Mr. F. had the effect of dissolving the first marriage. The decree of nullity granted by the state in reference to the second marriage cannot be regarded as having any validity according to the law of God for the simple reason that Scripture does not provide for this kind of annulment. Therefore the second marriage of Mr. F. is still to be regarded as existent and binding. For him to remarry the former Mrs. F. would be another act of adultery.

Index of Subjects

Adultery: death penalty in Old Testament, 10; only legitimate ground for divorce in New Testament, 42; no provision for divorce on this ground under Old Testament, 51

Analogy of marriage bond to the rule of the law, 78-95; shows binding character of marriage, 81, 90; not incompatible with legitimate divorce, 90-92

Bill of Divorcement: mandatory, 9, 20, 30

Cases: 110-117

Creation ordinance of marriage: did not permit divorce, 1, 31-33; presupposed by Paul, 64

Defilement and abomination of forbidden reunion, 13-15; not merely ceremonial, 13; not simply remarriage, 14; restoration after remarriage, 15

Desertion by unbelieving spouse: 67-69; severe judgment on, 68, 69; gives liberty to the deserted believer, 69-78

Divorce under Old Testament
Provision (see *Contents*): not mandatory, 3-7, 32, 44, 45; not legitimate, 6-8, 14, 15, 27; tolerated, 7, 8, 14, 15, 30, 32; intrinsically wrong, 8, 14, 28, 32; not the provision for adultery, 10, 27, 51; involved grave abnormalities, 13-15; discouraged, 14; allowed for remarriage, 14, 93; not tolerated by Christ, 28, 51; toleration occasioned by moral perversity, 30, 31; not in accord with the creation ordinance, 30-32; involved strict regulations, 45; alluded to by Paul, 92-95

Ecclesiastical divorce: 106-110

Fornication, the exceptive clause concerning: 33-43; applies to and allows remarriage, 43; omitted, 45, 46

Harmonization of passages: Jesus' teaching and the Old Testament provision, 44, 45; within the Gospels, 45-47, 51-54; textual variant considered, 47-50; Jesus' and Paul's teaching, 69-72, 89-92

Illegitimate Divorce: makes woman suffer adultery, 24; no right of remarriage, 25

Jesus' Teaching (see *Contents*): 17-54; not an abrogation of Old Testament law, 17, 28; not a relaxation of Old Testament obligation, 18, 28; inherent authority, 19, 27; abrogates particular penalties, 27, 28; abrogates previous toleration, 27, 28, 51; confirmation of Old Testament law, 28

Legitimate Divorce: adultery is only legitimate ground, 20, 21, 42; not mandatory even on proper ground, 21, 35; not provided for under Old Testament law, 27; instituted by Christ, 27; legitimizes remarriage, 33, 34, 52; Romish position on, 35-39, 55, 82, 83, 103-106; dissolves the marriage bond, 41-43; replaces the death penalty, 51; propriety of, 51, 52; rights of the woman regarding, 52-54; presupposes sanctity of marriage bond, 75; marriage dissolved by heinous desecration, 75

Marriage: ideally indissoluble, 1, 29, 31; bearing of sinful state on, 2, 75; unobliterable relationship involved, 14; not dissolved by illegitimate divorce, 25; divine ordinance, 29; dissolved by legitimate divorce, 41-43; for prevention of fornication, 57; debt, 57; covenant principle involved, 65; soteric implications if one partner is Christian, 65; sacred, 66, 67, 75; law of is binding, 72, 81, 90; may be dissolved for heinous desecration, 75

118

Index of Authors

Index of Scripture References